A PRACTICAL REFERENCE TO SNA

A PRACTICAL REFERENCE TO SNA

MIKE OXBORROW, BSc

McGRAW-HILL BOOK COMPANY
LONDON · NEW YORK · ST LOUIS · SAN FRANCISCO
AUCKLAND · BOGOTÁ · CARACAS · LISBON · MADRID
MEXICO · MILAN · MONTREAL · NEW DELHI
PANAMA · PARIS · SAN JUAN · SÃO PAULO
SINGAPORE · SYDNEY · TOKYO · TORONTO

Published by
McGRAW-HILL Book Company Europe
Shoppenhangers Road, Maidenhead,
Berkshire, SL6 2QL, England
Telephone 0628 23432
Fax 0628 770224

British Library Cataloguing in Publication Data
Oxborrow, Mike
    Practical Reference to SNA
    I. Title
    004.6
    ISBN 0-07-707791-1

Library of Congress Cataloging-in-Publication Data
Oxborrow, Mike
    A practical reference to SNA/Mike Oxborrow
        p.   cm.
    ISBN 0-07-707791-1
    1. SNA (Computer network architecture) I. Title.
    TK5105.5.093   1993
    004.6'5–dc20
                                        92-43138 CIP

Copyright © 1993 McGraw-Hill International (UK) Limited.
All rights reserved. No part of this publication may be reproduced, stored in a retrieval system, or transmitted, in any form or by any means, electronic, mechanical, photocopying, recording, or otherwise, without the prior permission of McGraw-Hill International (UK) Limited, with the exception of material entered and executed on a computer system for the reader's own use.

1234 CUP 9543

Typeset by Goodfellow & Egan Phototypesetting Ltd, Cambridge, and printed and bound in Cambridge at the University Press

This book is dedicated to Gill Jefferies who taught me how to string a sentence together. It was a very difficult job.

And of course to Felice.

CONTENTS

Preface   xiii

Active, activation   1
Addressing   1
APPC   2
Application to application sessions   2
APPN   2
APPN end node   3
APPN network node   3
Approach to the definitions   4
Architecture and implementation   4
Asynchronous support   5
AS/400   5
Basic definitions   7
The BIND command   7
BIU   8
BLU   8
Boundary function   9
Brackets   9
BTU   10
CDRM   10
CDRSC   11
Chaining   12
Channels   13
CICS   14
Class of service   14
Cluster controllers   15
Communication controller node   15
Control points   15
Conversations   16
CPIC   16
Cross-domain networking   17
Cross-domain LU-LU session setup   17
Domains   18
ELLC   18

End users   19
Explicit routes   20
FAP manual   20
FEP   20
File transfer   20
Frames   21
Function management headers   22
Function management profiles   22
Half sessions   23
Hierarchy   24
Host node   25
IND$FILE   25
JES   26
Jokes   26
Layers   27
Layers—an alternative view   27
LEN end node   28
Links   28
Link header   28
Link stations   29
Link trailer   29
Local address   29
Logical units   30
Logical unit types   31
Logmodes   32
Loose talk   32
LU-LU sessions   33
LU6.2   34
Mainframes   34
Mainframe structure   35
Major node   37
Minor node   37
MSNF   37
NAU   37
NCCF   38
NCP   38
Netview   38
Netview command facility   39
Netview compatibility   39
Netview hardware monitor   40
Netview performance monitor   40

Netview session monitor 40
Netview status monitor 40
Network address 41
Network management 43
Network solicitors 44
NJE 45
Node 45
NPA 46
NPDA 46
NPSI 46
NPSI overhead 48
NRZ and NRZI 49
NTO 49
Pacing 50
Parallel LU-LU sessions 52
Peer-to-peer 52
PEP 53
Performance problems 53
Peripheral nodes 54
Physical units 54
PIU 55
Primary LU 55
Printing 55
Problems 56
Protocol conversion 57
PU2.1 58
QLLC 59
Requests 61
Request headers 61
Request modes—immediate and delayed 61
Request units 61
Responses 62
Response headers 62
Response modes—definite, exception and none 63
Response modes—immediate and delayed 64
Response times 64
Response units 65
RH 65
RTM 66
RU 66
SAA 66

Contents

SDLC 67
SDLC control field 68
SDLC or X25? 70
Secondary LU 71
Segmenting 71
Sense data 72
Sequences 72
Sessions 72
Session level pacing 73
Session types 73
SNA—what exactly is it? 74
SNI 74
Spoofing 75
SSCP 76
Standard systems 76
Starting a printer session 78
Starting a terminal session 78
Station address 79
Subareas 79
Subarea node 80
System request key 81
S/3X 81
TH 81
Token ring 82
Traffic volumes 82
Transaction 83
Transaction program 83
Transmission group 83
Transmission headers 84
Transmission priority 85
TSO 85
Tuning 86
Units of data 86
USS 88
USS commands 88
USS messages 89
USS tables 90
Virtual routes 91
Virtual route pacing 91
VM 91
VTAM 91

Contents   xi

VTAM applications   92
VTAM commands   93
VTAM datasets   93
VTAM states   94
XIDs   94
X25   95
3270 system   95
5250 system   95

Appendices

A   IBM manuals   97
B   Common sequences   99
C   Common IBM communications hardware   106
D   Common SNA commands   107

PREFACE

This book is a mixture of SNA theory, how things work in practice, and other information that is required to perform SNA networking in the real world. It concentrates on traditional hierarchical SNA. APPN and other products that constitute the future in SNA networking are discussed briefly. To cover the APPN and APPC in any reasonable depth would double the size of this book. However, many of the terms and concepts covered in this book are applicable to the future of SNA.

The language is deliberately simple within the constraints of technical accuracy. The words 'lump' and 'thing' are deliberately used in places where IBM already uses more sensible words to mean something specific. The meaning should be apparent from the context. If you want to read phrases like 'formal temporary bilateral', or 'geographic and temporal proximities' you have bought the wrong book.

If you are new or newish to SNA, it would be helpful to read the section on 'approach to the definitions', the section 'SNA—what exactly is it?' and then the section on 'basic definitions'.

If you are familiar with SNA, and would like information on a particular subject, look it up in the contents pages and go directly to it. Each section has words that are in bold type. This means that the subject is covered in a dedicated section.

This book does not cover all the available information. Definitive and complete information comes only from the relevant IBM manual. There is a list of the most useful manuals in Appendix A.

What I have tried to do with this book is produce something that is of practical use to people trying to work with SNA in a commercial environment. The idea is that each subject is easy to find and that it will only take a few minutes to understand the important points. I hope that I have succeeded.

Active, activation

Those who are reading this book alphabetically will be horrified to find that the first subject has two different meanings depending on the context. This is not common.

Meaning 1

A **session** is active if it is in existence. So if an **SSCP** is in session with a **PU**, then the SSCP-PU session is active.

Meaning 2

Active and activation also relate to **VTAM**. VTAM **major** and minor **nodes** are brought into service using the VTAM command VARY ACTIVE. This is known as varying the resource active, or activating the resource. Once a particular resource has been successfully activated, then its VTAM state will be ACTIV(sic).

Sometimes the two meanings coincide. For example, if we activate an LU (meaning 2) successfully, then the LU-SSCP session will be active (meaning 1). This, however, is not the case for activation (meaning 2) of a major node, as there is no such thing as a session with a major node.

Addressing

There are three different addresses that we can talk about in an **SNA** network. They are:

1. The *network address*. This is the address of an **NAU** in the network. It uniquely defines the NAU in the network.
2. The *station address*. This is sometimes called the poll address, **SDLC** address, or **cluster** address; although only **station address** is strictly correct. This is the address by which one end of an SDLC circuit polls another. See the section entitled 'SDLC' for more details.
3. The *local address*. This points to a particular terminal on a **cluster controller**, or whether the data has come from the **SSCP** or an application.

- *subarea nodes* use the network address
- *peripheral nodes* use the local address
- *SDLC* uses the station address

APPC

APPC stands for advanced program to program communication. APPC defines a set of verbs for program to program communication in much the same way that 3270 defines a set of commands for program to terminal communication. APPC and **LU6.2** have a relationship equivalent to 3270 and LU2. This means that APPC is often used as a synonym for LU6.2, although this is not strictly correct.

Application to application sessions

Broadly speaking, there are two types of application to application **session**—**LU6.2** and all the rest. This section only considers all the rest. The most common ones are **JES**-JES (used for shipping batch data around the network) and **CICS**-CICS (used to pass database requests). Once they are **active**, there is nothing particularly special about an application to application session. Instead of one end of the session being in a terminal and one in a **mainframe**, both ends are in a mainframe. The mechanism for starting an application to application session is similar to starting an application to printer session. The first thing that we would see if we had a datascope in the correct place would be a **BIND command** activating the session. The session type is usually 6.1, although this depends on the applications.

Application to application sessions are usually **cross-domain**, although it is possible to have a same domain application to application session. All the SNA commands would flow within the host, however, so this case is not really relevant to the network.

APPN

APPN stands for advanced peer-to-peer networking. APPN is a set of SNA rules that cover networking. APPN is important as it is IBM's strategic direction for the future of SNA.

The important point about APPN is that it solves most of the problems and difficulties associated with traditional hierarchical networking. The only PU type used in APPN is **PU2.1**, so all sessions can be **peer-to-peer**. APPN offers the following advantages over hierarchical SNA:

1. Dynamic definitions are the norm rather than the exception. This simplifies network reconfiguration and expansion.

2. All IBM hardware platforms implement APPN. Therefore, combining different systems in a single network should be a comparatively straightforward exercise.

APPN is designed to work closely with **LU6.2**, so it is unlikely that APPN networks will be seen with LUs other than 6.2.

IBM licenses the APPN network node code to other manufacturers. The idea of this is to make it easier for other manufacturers to implement APPN on their systems.

Another important point to remember about APPN is that it is part of SNA, not instead of SNA. This means that APPN networks can work successfully with hierarchical SNA networks, although this usually results in the loss of some of the APPN functionality.

See also the sections on **APPN end node**, **APPN network node** and **LEN end node**.

APPN end node

The APPN end node has the middle functionality of the three types of T2.1 node types.

The main functionality of the APPN end node is as follows:

1. Some directory and routeing facilities for LUs on the node are available, but with less capability than the **APPN network node**. **Peer-to-peer LU-LU sessions** are only supported when the associated T2.1 nodes are adjacent.
2. LUs attached to the APPN end node can be registered with an APPN network node that acts as a server. This gives the LUs access to peer-to-peer **sessions** across the entire APPN network.
3. Attachment to multiple network nodes is allowed, but only one CP-CP session is supported.
4. CP-CP sessions are not allowed to be active to other APPN end nodes. Together with the above restriction on a single CP-CP session to a network node, this means that the APPN end node is heavily dependent on the APPN network node.

APPN network node

The APPN network node is the most functional of the three types of T2.1 **node** types.

The main functionality of the network node is as follows:

1. Multiple CP-CP **sessions**.

2. Comprehensive directory and routeing facilities for LUs on the network node and also for all LUs attached to adjacent **LEN end nodes** or **APPN end nodes**. The network node must be acting as a server to the LEN end nodes or APPN end nodes using a CP-CP session.
3. Routeing of data on an **LU-LU session**, where neither LU is in the APPN network node. This is called intermediate session routeing.
4. Network management functions.

Approach to the definitions

The most important thing that must be done with SNA definitions and words is to remember and apply them. This may sound obvious, but many people try to use analogies to help them 'understand'. This invariably leads to confusion sooner or later, so avoid it if possible. The people most likely to get confused are OSI experts, as they look for the equivalencies between OSI and SNA. An SNA definition is like a mathematical one in that it tells us which words to use to describe a particular part of our system, or how the system interacts.

Try to accept the system for what it is. Thinking about how badly SNA is designed, or how inefficient it is will not help you to learn about it. SNA just is. Whatever we may think about it, it is still arguably the most successful networking architecture around today, and if you are reading this book, understanding SNA will help you do your job.

Architecture and implementation

SNA is a set of rules covering IBM communications. However, manufacturers, including IBM, interpret these rules differently, and also implement different sets of rules and functionality on products that do the same job. Let us look at the following examples in the **3270 system**.

The SNA rules according to the **FAP manual** include a definition for the PU2. That definition includes a downline load capability which the 3174 does not support, although the 3174 is considered to be a true PU2.

There are various ways in which the architecture allows a **cluster controller** to clear up if a terminal is powered off in mid-**session**. Different products implement this clearing up function in different ways. For example, we could send a RSHUTD, or an **UNBIND** or a logoff message, on the **SSCP**-LU session. All are perfectly legal according to the rules.

Problems sometimes arise if products do not implement the rules as we expect. A common example is in the way applications process the LUSTAT command when it has been sent to indicate a terminal problem. Some applications will wait until the terminal is available, and restart the **LU-LU session** at the point where the problem was first noticed. Other applications will effectively log the user off. To summarize, different products may behave in different ways, but still conform to the SNA rules.

Asynchronous support

The first point which needs to be considered when connecting asynchronous terminals to an IBM system is what **session type** do we want to support. If session type 2 or 7 is required, then **protocol conversion** must be used. However, for session type 1, which is effectively TTY, we can connect directly to the **FEP**. To do this we need extra software to support the non-IBM protocol. If asynchronous support is to be used directly, then **NTO** (network terminal option) must be used. The alternative is to use an **X25** PAD, and bring the terminals in using X25. **NPSI** (network packet switching interface) is required here.

An alternative to NTO or NPSI if session type 1 is required, is to use a protocol converter that supports conversion to LU1. This would look to the IBM host like a 3767 device. The advantage of this approach is that neither NTO nor NPSI is required, and the approach gives us a more **standard system**.

AS/400

The AS/400 is IBM's mid-range machine. It comes in various sizes ranging from large PC to small **mainframe** (Fig. 1). There are three most common ways in which the AS/400 is attached to a network. We will consider each separately.

3270 emulation

Here the AS/400 emulates a 3174 **cluster controller**. It is attached to an FEP. Users wishing to start an **LU-LU session** on the mainframe select the appropriate option from a menu. The system behaves exactly like a 3174 from an SNA point of view. The AS/400 will be the secondary **SDLC** station in this case.

AS/400

3270 emulation

```
[AS/400]—[M]~[M]—[FEP]
```

looks like

```
[3 x 74]—[M]~[M]—[FEP]
```

Acting as a host

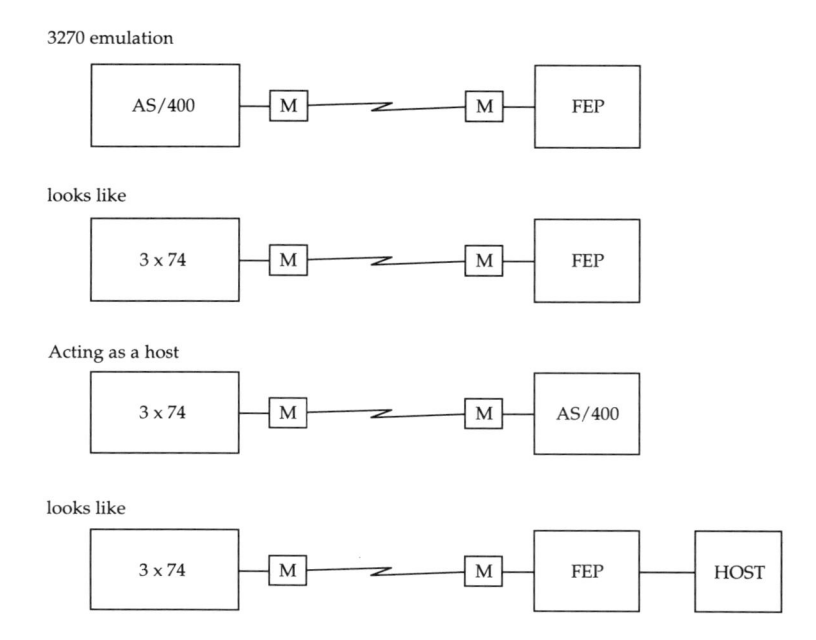

```
[3 x 74]—[M]~[M]—[AS/400]
```

looks like

```
[3 x 74]—[M]~[M]—[FEP]—[HOST]
```

Figure 1   AS/400 communications examples

Acting as a host

In this mode, the AS/400 controls the cluster controller—either a **3270** or **5250**. It is important to remember that a 5250 system is controlled differently from a 3270 system. The reason is that the PU types are different. The AS/400 will be the primary **SDLC** station in this case.

Acting as a node type 2.1

In this mode, the AS/400 supports **PU2.1**, and talks to other 2.1s or PU4s. Depending on the AS/400 configuration, it can support various subsets of the functionality including **APPN**.

Hints and tips

While the AS/400 will support 3270 terminal systems if required, it is designed for 5250. In order to support 3270, an internal translation from 3270 to 5250 is performed. This leads to various complications which means that running 3270 on an AS/400 is usually more trouble than it is worth.

SDLC is implemented much more rigorously than the 3745. This can cause problems with certain IBM-compatible equipment.

When acting as a host to a 3270 cluster controller, what would appear to be the **SSCP** banner actually comes from an application.

Error recovery and retry limits are governed by system as well as communication parameters.

The communications processing is done by the main processor. If the communication parameters are set carelessly, this can lead to a significant proportion of the processor being used for inefficient communications. This can lead to poor application **response times**.

Basic definitions

The following are the basic definitions which must be learnt before tackling SNA:

- **end user**
- **LU**
- **PU**
- **SSCP**
- **session**

Read the sections covering the definitions above and try to memorize them. The trick is not to try to understand what they mean or where they are, but aim to apply the definition without thinking too much. The people who have most problems are usually more experienced, and try to analogize the SNA definitions with something that they are familiar with. This should be avoided at all costs.

You will probably forget the definitions. When that happens, go back to the relevant page and re-read the definition. It will stick in your mind eventually, so persevere.

The BIND command

The BIND command actually starts (or activates to use the correct terminology) the **LU-LU session**. It flows from one LU to the other. The LU that sends the BIND is defined as the **primary LU** (PLU) and the LU that receives the BIND is defined as the **secondary LU** (SLU).

The BIND contains descriptions of the **session** which are called session parameters. Information contained in the BIND includes **session type**, maximum **RU** size allowed and **pacing** information.

BINDs can be either negotiable or non-negotiable. If the secondary LU does not like the BIND parameters, one of two things will happen. If the BIND is negotiable, then the SLU will send back a revised BIND, and the two LUs will then negotiate a mutually agreeable BIND if possible. If the BIND is non-negotiable, then the SLU will reject the bind.

In a **VTAM** system, the BIND image is contained in VTAM tables called **logmode** tables. Each logmode table entry contains the BIND image in hexadecimal. However, care must be taken as sometimes the logmode table entry will be overridden by other definitions. Some of the **NCP** definitions will do this, and **CICS** can also cause this problem. If you ever suspect a problem with the BIND image used, it is a good idea to trace the BIND to check exactly what is being sent.

BIU

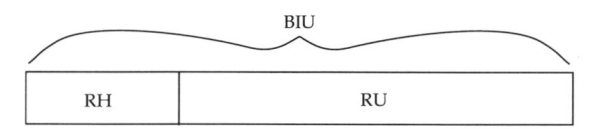

```
                         BIU
        ┌─────────────────────────────────────┐
        │   RH    │            RU             │
        └─────────┴───────────────────────────┘
```

Figure 2   BIU format

BIU stands for basic information unit. A BIU is an **RH** followed by an **RU** (Fig. 2). The BIU does not specify whether the RU is a **request** or a **response**. See also the section on **units of data**.

BLU

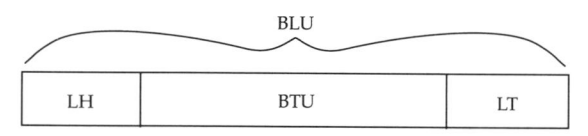

```
                         BLU
        ┌─────────────────────────────────────┐
        │  LH   │         BTU         │  LT   │
        └───────┴─────────────────────┴───────┘
```

Figure 3   BLU format

BLU stands for basic link unit. A BLU is a **BTU** enclosed in a **link header** and **link trailer**. The BLU is the lump of data which is sent across the **link** in one piece (Fig. 3). See also the section on **units of data**.

Boundary function

The boundary function resides in **subarea nodes** (PU4s and PU5s). It provides support for downstream **peripheral nodes**.

To take an example, consider a 3174 attached to a 3745. The boundary function translates the **network address**, used by the 3745, to the **local address**, used by the **cluster controller**.

Brackets

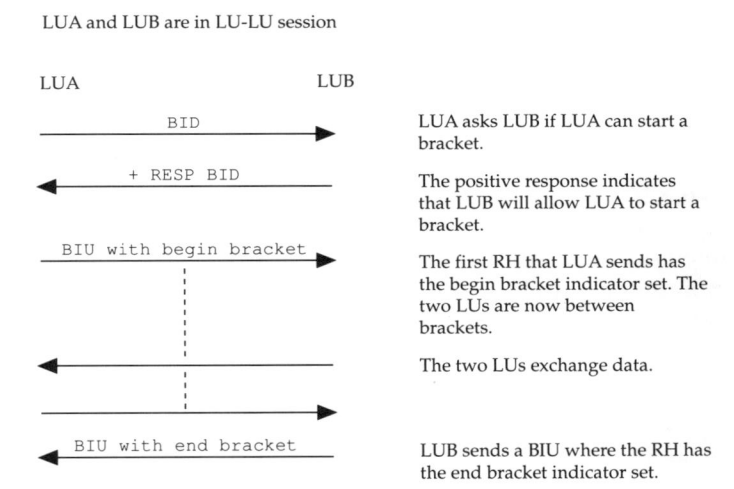

LUA and LUB are in LU-LU session

```
LUA                              LUB
         BID
    ─────────────────▶              LUA asks LUB if LUA can start a
                                    bracket.
         + RESP BID
    ◀─────────────────              The positive response indicates
                                    that LUB will allow LUA to start a
                                    bracket.
    BIU with begin bracket
    ─────────────────▶              The first RH that LUA sends has
                                    the begin bracket indicator set. The
                                    two LUs are now between
                                    brackets.

    ◀─────────────────              The two LUs exchange data.
    ─────────────────▶

    BIU with end bracket
    ◀─────────────────              LUB sends a BIU where the RH has
                                    the end bracket indicator set.
```

Figure 4   Example of a bracket

A bracket is a sequence of **requests** and **responses** exchanged between two **logical units** (Fig. 4). The sequence can be in one or both directions. The start of a bracket is indicated by a begin bracket indicator in the **request header**, and the end by an end bracket indicator, also in the request header.

Bracket protocol is a method for grouping chains of **BIUs** into one logical unit of work from the point of view of the **end user**. Bracket protocol controls which LU is able to send data at a particular time by defining a first speaker and a bidder. This is done as part of the **BIND**. The first speaker can start a bracket whenever it likes, but the bidder must ask for permission, typically by sending a BID. Alternatively, the two LUs can use contention to initiate a bracket. BIU chains can be sent in both directions within a bracket, the change direction indicator being used to control this.

BTU

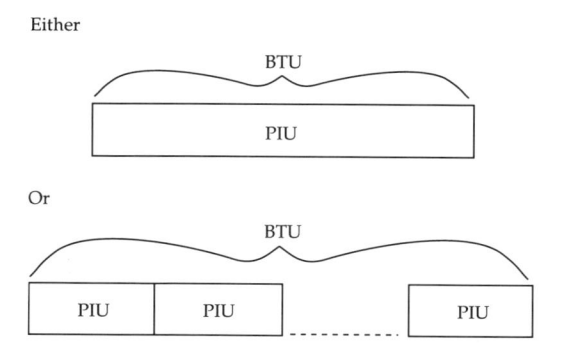

Either

```
            BTU
    ┌─────────────────┐
    │       PIU       │
    └─────────────────┘
```

Or

```
              BTU
  ┌─────┬─────┐        ┌─────┐
  │ PIU │ PIU │ ------ │ PIU │
  └─────┴─────┘        └─────┘
```

Figure 5   BTU format

BTU stands for basic transmission unit. A BTU is either a **PIU** or multiple PIUs blocked together (Fig. 5). Blocking occurs if the **link** parameters are set such that the maximum **BLU** size is large enough to accommodate multiple PIUs. In this case, blocking results in more efficient data transfer across the link. See also the section on units of data.

CDRM

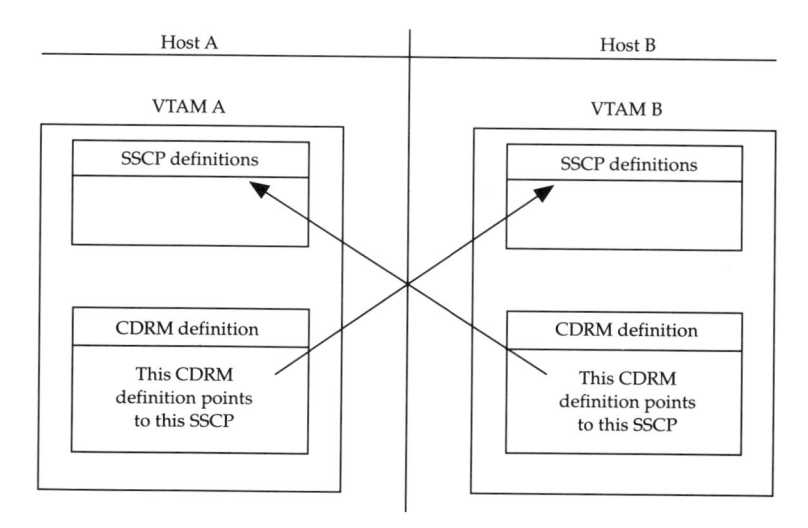

```
          Host A                    |           Host B
          VTAM A                    |           VTAM B
  ┌──────────────────────┐          |   ┌──────────────────────┐
  │   SSCP definitions   │◄──┐      |   │   SSCP definitions   │◄──┐
  │                      │   │      |   │                      │   │
  └──────────────────────┘   │      |   └──────────────────────┘   │
                             │      |                              │
  ┌──────────────────────┐   │      |   ┌──────────────────────┐   │
  │   CDRM definition    │   │      |   │   CDRM definition    │   │
  │     This CDRM        │───┼──────┼───│     This CDRM        │───┘
  │  definition points   │   └──────┼───│  definition points   │
  │   to this SSCP       │          |   │   to this SSCP       │
  └──────────────────────┘          |   └──────────────────────┘
```

Figure 6   CDRMs — two-domain example

CDRM stands for cross-domain resource manager. A CDRM is a **VTAM** definition, which defines another **SSCP**, so that by using CDRM definitions, two or more VTAMs can know about each other (Fig. 6).

When the relevant CDRMs are activated, an SSCP-SSCP session is activated. This means that the two VTAMs are talking to each other, and can exchange information using cross-domain **LU-LU session requests**.

CDRSC

```
                    Host A              |              Host B
                    VTAM A              |              VTAM B
         ┌────────────────────────┐     |     ┌────────────────────────┐
         │   CDRSC definition     │     |     │   CDRSC definition     │
         │ This CDRSC definition  │     |     │ This CDRSC definition  │
         │ points to this LU. It was    |     │ points to this LU.     │
         │ probably pre-defined   │     |     │ It was probably        │
         │                        │     |     │ dynamically defined    │
         └────────────────────────┘     |     └────────────────────────┘

         Terminal                                     Application
                                                      CICS for example
```

This is the cross-domain LU-LU session that is active

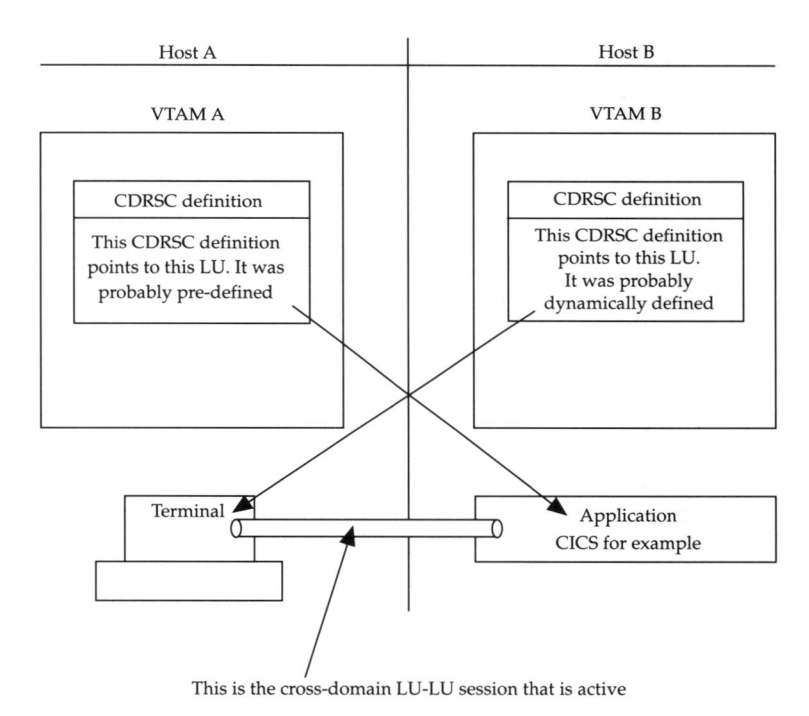

Figure 7   CDRSCs—two-domain example

CDRSC stands for cross-domain resource. A CDRSC is a **VTAM** definition, which defines an LU that is in another **domain** (Fig. 7).

When a CDRSC definition has been activated successfully, this means that the VTAM concerned now knows about an LU that is not in its domain. This means that when a **request** for an **LU-LU session** is received, VTAM knows where the requested resource is, even though it may not be in its domain.

Chaining

For a **cross-domain LU-LU session** to be active, CDRSC definitions for both LUs must exist. VTAM has the capability to generate some of these definitions dynamically, and this is typically done for terminal LUs. Application LUs are usually pre-defined.

Chaining

Single element chain

| RH | RU |

Begin chain indicator set.
End chain indicator set.

Multiple element chain

| RH | RU |

Begin chain indicator set.

| RH | RU |
| RH | RU |

Neither begin chain indicator nor end chain indicator set.

| RH | RU |

End chain indicator set.

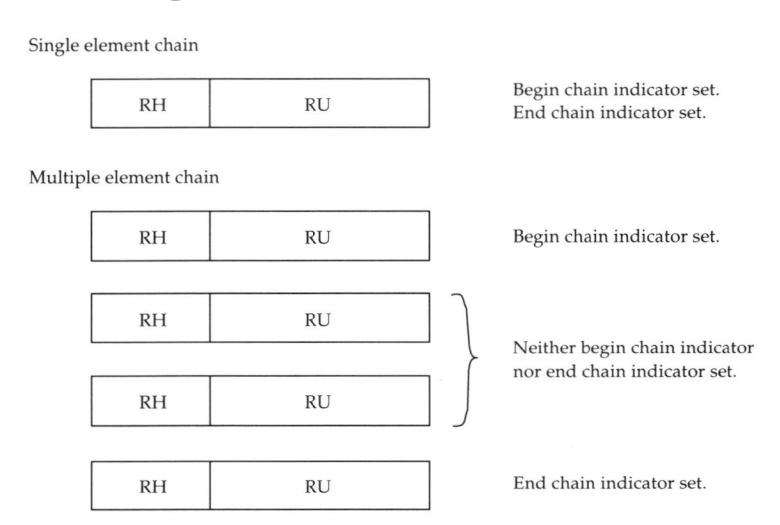

Figure 8   Chains

A chain is a sequence of **BIUs** sent from one LU to another that constitute a single transfer of data (Fig. 8). A chain is unidirectional.

The point of chaining protocol is that the two LUs process the chain as if it had been sent as one lump of data. Error recovery can be handled on a per chain basis as can **responses** (Fig. 9).

Chaining is commonly used in **3270 systems**, where a single 3270 screen will be sent as a chain of multiple BIUs. The **RH** contains a begin chain indicator and an end chain indicator. By examining these bits, we can tell whether an **RU** is the beginning, middle or end RU in the chain. It is possible to have a chain containing a single RU. In this case, both the begin chain indicator and end chain indicator bits will be set.

Channels

Say a 3270 application sends a screen of data as three BIUs in a single chain:

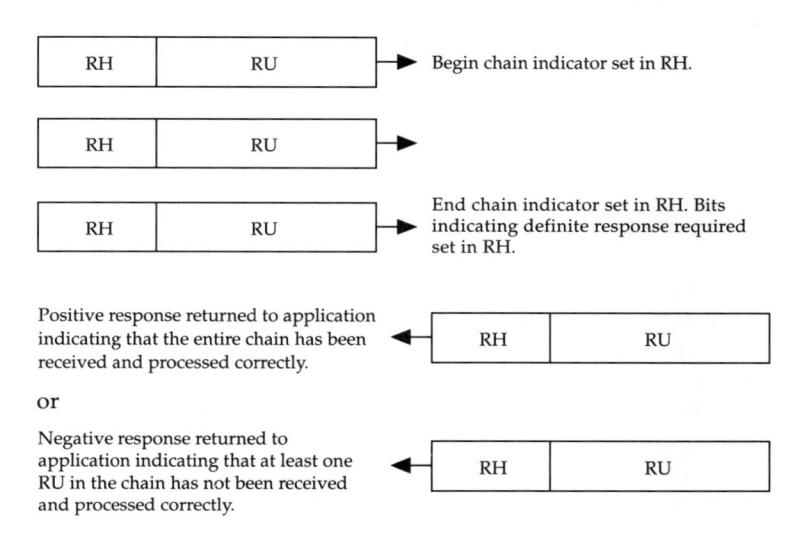

| RH | RU | → Begin chain indicator set in RH. |

| RH | RU | → |

| RH | RU | → End chain indicator set in RH. Bits indicating definite response required set in RH. |

Positive response returned to application indicating that the entire chain has been received and processed correctly. ← | RH | RU |

or

Negative response returned to application indicating that at least one RU in the chain has not been received and processed correctly. ← | RH | RU |

If a negative response is received, then the application re-sends the entire chain.

Figure 9   Use of chaining example

Channels

A channel is the system for connecting a **mainframe** computer to its peripherals. The two peripherals of interest from a communications standpoint are the **FEP** and the channel-attached 3174 (remember that the 3174 can be channel, **link** or **token** ring attached).

IBM mainframes will typically have many channel ports. Channel-attached devices are daisy-chained from a particular port.

Channels run typically at several megabits per second, so usually the channel is irrelevant to performance in a properly designed system. However, if a 3745 shares a channel with a number of other busy peripherals, then channel delay may be a significant factor in network performance.

Channels can be extended over high-speed circuits, so it is possible to have channel connections extending over great distances if requirements allow.

Mainframes can be attached to each other using channel to channel connections if required.

CICS

CICS (customer information control system) is a general purpose transaction processing monitor. Its purpose is to act as an interface between the user-written application programs and the network. CICS interfaces to user applications on one side, and **VTAM** on the other.

The application LU and other SNA functionality is provided by CICS. A typical CICS system will have **3270** applications and LU1 printing.

CICS is table driven, in classical IBM fashion. The most important table from a communications point of view is the TCT or terminal control table. The TCT contains CICS terminal entries, as CICS terminals are known by CICS names. Each CICS terminal has a corresponding VTAM name, as defined in the VTAM tables. The TCT contains this match. The TCT can also contain a **logmode** entry that will override all other entries. This can lead to problems where a logmode is coded in the **NCP**, but CICS overrides this and does its own thing.

In the latest releases of CICS, the TCT can now be built dynamically, which in theory removes the need to pre-define all the terminals manually.

Class of service

Each **LU-LU session** will have a class of service associated with it. The class of service specifies the performance characteristics that will be used when routeing **session** data between **subareas**. It includes the **transmission priority** and the choice of routes that are available to the session. The class of service to be used in an LU-LU session is pointed at by the **logmode**.

Classes of service are contained in a class of service table, or COS table. The COS table contains all the defined classes of service for a network. Each COS table entry reflects a particular set of end user needs.

For example, there are three different sets of end users in the network:

1. *Production on-line*: it is important that we give them good **response times** and availability. Therefore the production on-line class of service points to the highest transmission priority and gives the widest possible choice for routeing.

2. *Development on-line*: requirements are similar here, but the service is not as important as production. So we use the middle transmission priority and restrict the possible choices for routeing.
3. *Batch*: this traffic is sent on the lowest transmission priority, as response time is not critical. Some alternative routes are allowed, but less than development on-line.

The COS table contains a number of COS table entries, each entry lists the number of **virtual routes** and transmission priorities available to LU-LU sessions using that particular entry.

Cluster controllers

Cluster controllers are devices that act as the interface between a number of terminal devices and a communications **link**. There are two main systems: the **3270 system** and the **5250 system**.

Communication controller node

A communication controller node is communications controller hardware (for example, a 3745) with a network control program (for example, ACF/**NCP**) running in it. The definition is rather circular, but for practical purposes, a communications controller node is an IBM 37XX with NCP or hardware and software that provides equivalent functionality.

Communications controller node is usually shortened to COMC. Sometimes called a communications controller subarea node, a COMC is one of the two types of **subarea node**.

Control points

The control point (CP) is responsible for managing the resources of a T2.1 node. It is similar in concept to **SSCP**. CPs communicate with other CPs using CP-CP **sessions**. The major components of CP are listed below:

1. *Configuration services* manage the **links** to adjacent **nodes**.
2. *Topology and routeing services* manage information on the network topology, and provide routeing information on **LU-LU sessions**.
3. *Directory services* are responsible for locating network resources.

4. *Session services* are responsible for controlling CP-CP and LU-LU sessions.
5. *Management services* monitor and control the resources of the node.

Conversations

Figure 10   Conversations and sessions

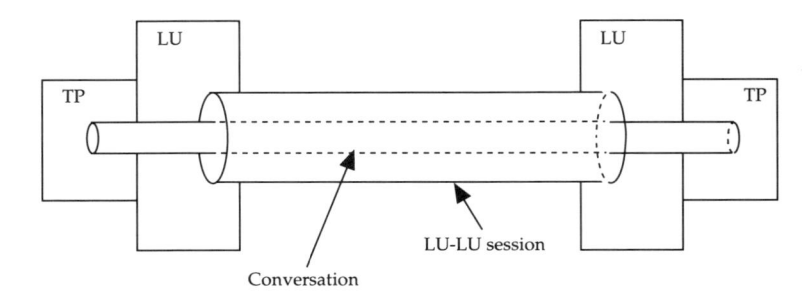

LU – logical unit
TP – transaction program

A conversation is a logical connection between **transaction programs** (Fig. 10). Transaction programs communicate over conversations in much the same way that **logical units** communicate over **sessions**. A particular session can only have one conversation active on it at any one time, so conversations happen serially over a session. If two transaction programs require more than one conversation to be simultaneously active, then one **parallel LU-LU session** must be active for each simultaneous conversation.

CPIC

CPIC stands for common programming interface communications. It contains a standard set of application program calls that will allow program to program communication. CPIC uses **LU6.2** to provide session services.

CPIC provides all the functionality to start and stop a **conversation** and send and receive data between programs. This means that any CPIC compliant application should be able to communicate with any other CPIC compliant application. Whether the two applications that are communicating will be able to do any useful work depends on the part of the applications that actually process the data, but that is not a CPIC issue.

CPIC is one of the standards included in **SAA**, which means that it is significant.

Cross-domain networking

Session startup is easy when both LUs that want to start a session are in the same **domain**. There is an **SSCP**-LU session for both LUs, so when a **request** for an **LU-LU session** arrives at the SSCP, it has all the information required to process the session request.

When the network contains multiple domains, an additional mechanism is required to enable cross-domain LU-LU sessions. The SSCP that receives the LU-LU session request is not in session with the requested LU, therefore it does not know anything about it.

To overcome these problems, the SSCPs communicate over SSCP-SSCP sessions. Information on a cross-domain LU-LU session can now be passed between SSCPs. SNA defines cross-domain resource managers (**CDRMs**) and cross-domain resources (**CDRSCs**) to perform this communication.

Once the SSCP-SSCP session is started and the relevant CDRSCs are active we are in a position to start a cross-domain session.

See also the sections on **cross-domain LU-LU session setup** and **MSNF**.

Cross-domain LU-LU session setup

It is important to remember that any **request** from an LU for a **session** goes to the **SSCP** that owns it. A common misconception is that the **communication controller node** traps the logon request and sends it to the SSCP that owns the requested application. This is *not* the case.

The sequence of commands for cross-domain session setup is given in Appendix B. An example of network topology is given in Fig. 11.

Once the **LU-LU session** has been activated, the SSCP that is in session with the terminal takes no part in data transfer. In fact the terminal's SSCP can go down without affecting the LU-LU session in most cases.

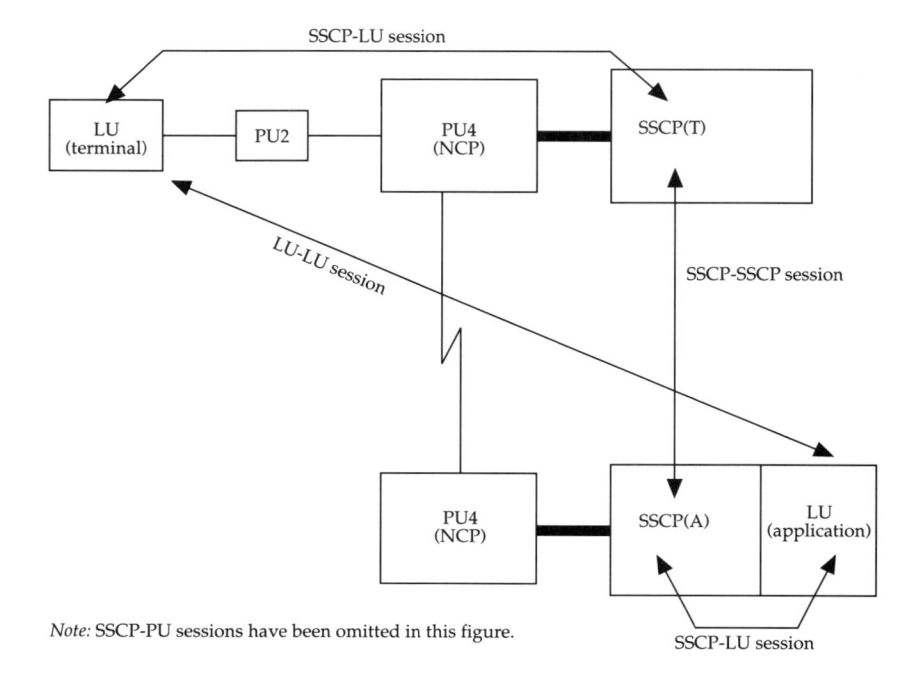

Figure 11 Cross-domain networking example — topology and sessions required

Domains

Domain is a term used to define an area of control (Fig. 12). In **mainframe** networking, a domain is an **SSCP** and all the resources that it controls: terminals, **NCPs**, applications, etc.

In **APPN** networking, a domain is a **control point**, and all the resources that it controls.

ELLC

ELLC stands for enhanced logical link control. ELLC provides direct **X25** support for SNA devices in much the same way as **QLLC**.

ELLC provides additional end to end acknowledgement, which gives greater integrity of data transfer between **link stations**. In a reasonably reliable network, the additional protocol overhead outweighs the benefit of additional integrity, so ELLC is not often used.

ELLC should only be used in an unreliable network. However, the real solution is to make the network more reliable.

End users 19

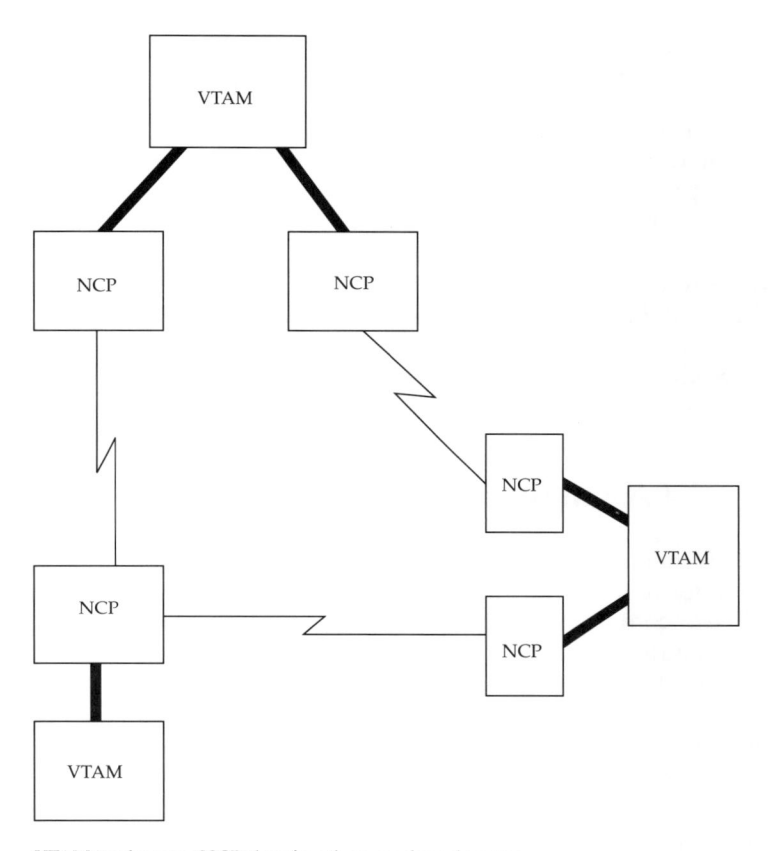

VTAM implements SSCP, therefore there are three domains.

Figure 12   Example of a network with three domains

End users

All computer networks have sources of and destinations for data. In SNA these sources and destinations are called end users.

A terminal was an end user, until IBM started moving SNA functionality into it. Now, only some terminals can be considered end users. However, the person sitting at the terminal is definitely an end user.

End users are not SNA resources—simply the source or destination of network data.

The point at which the end user stops and the SNA network starts is a rather grey area. Luckily it does not really matter.

Explicit routes

Explicit routes or ERs define a physical route between **subareas**. An explicit route is defined as an ordered set of subareas and **transmission groups**. The ERs are assigned numbers from 0 to 15. If an ER is defined from subarea x to subarea y, then there must be another ER defined from subarea y to subarea x. The same set of subareas and transmission groups must be used for the reverse explicit route, but a different ER number can be used. This is not recommended, but sometimes the network configuration can force this.

Explicit routes, **virtual routes** and **transmission priorities** are together used to define the **class of service**.

FAP manual

The format and protocols (FAP) manual contains definitive details of the logic and architecture for all of SNA apart from LU6.x and **PU2.1**. It also contains details of the structure of the data flows and commands.

Everything you need to know for implementing SNA (except LU6.x and PU2.1) is contained in this manual, so it can be argued that SNA is an open architecture. Only the architecture is discussed; it does not include any specific implementations (see the section on **architecture and implementation**). The manual is about four inches thick, and somewhat turgid. Similar information is contained in various other manuals, details of which are given in Appendix A.

FEP

FEP stands for front end processor. An FEP is simply a **communication controller node** which is **channel**-attached to a **mainframe**.

It is common practice, although incorrect, to use FEP to refer to any communication controller node. The important point is that the SNA functionality of a communication controller node is independent of whether it has a channel connection or not.

File transfer

File transfer is often done as an integral part of an interactive system, which means that files will be transferred on the same **session** as normal interactive data. So we have large volumes of file transfer data competing for network resources at the same priority as interactive data. This can lead to **performance problems** in badly thought out systems. There are three **session types** that are normally used for file transfer:

LU1

The data stream is effectively 'block of data then next block of data . . .', so LU1 is well suited to file transfer.

LU2

This method of transfer can be thought of as a fast typist filling the screen and then hitting the enter key for upload, or a fast reader reading the 3270 screen and then hitting enter for download. The data stream is 3270, which contains screen **addressing** and control. This is additional to the data that is being 'file transferred', so there is an associated overhead with this method. It is used when the user already has a 3270 session, for example running file transfer from a **TSO** ISPF menu.

LU6.2

As LU6.2 is independent of the datastream, it can also be used for file transfer.

Network tuning parameters can make a big difference to data throughput when doing file transfer. The following parameters are some that should be considered:

- maximum **RU** size
- **link** protocol **frame** size
- link protocol frame window size
- **SDLC** poll pause
- application priority
- line speed
- PC processing time
- **pacing**

The two main file transfer protocols supplied by IBM are **IND$FILE** and OSI/FTF.

Frames

'Frame' means the same as **SDLC BLU**, i.e. a single SDLC transmission that starts and ends with a flag. The problem is that 'frame' tends to be used for any particular unit of data transmission, for example 'the application sends a screen as two frames'. This leads to confusion, so my advice is to avoid using the term frame except in the context of **X25**.

See also the section on **loose talk**.

Function management headers

A function management (FM) header is an optional field at the beginning of an **RU** or RU **chain**. It carries control information for the LU. FM headers are most commonly used now in **LU6.2** sessions, but are also used in batch **sessions** in order to control the ultimate destination of the data.

Function management profiles

A function management (FM) profile is a particular set of protocols that will be used by the data flow control layer (see the section on **layers**). A **session** will have a particular FM profile associated with it. This is agreed using the **BIND command**, the FM profile is denoted by a number and is contained in byte 2.

The FM profile is one of the parameters defined by the **LU-LU session** type.

Example of FM profiles

For session type 2 FM profile 3 is used. It specifies the following:

1. **Primary LU half session** and **secondary LU half session** use immediate **response mode**.
2. Primary LU half session and secondary LU half session support the following DFC functions:
   CANCEL
   SIG
   LUSTAT
   CHASE
   SHUTD
   SHUTC
   RSHUTD
   BID and RTR (only if brackets are used)

The FM usage fields defining the options are:

- **chaining** usage

- request control mode selection
- chain response protocol
- compression indicator
- send end bracket indicator
- FM header usage
- brackets usage and re-set state
- bracket termination rule
- alternative code set allowed indicator
- normal flow send/receive mode
- recovery responsibility
- contention winner/loser
- half duplex flip-flop re-set states

Half sessions

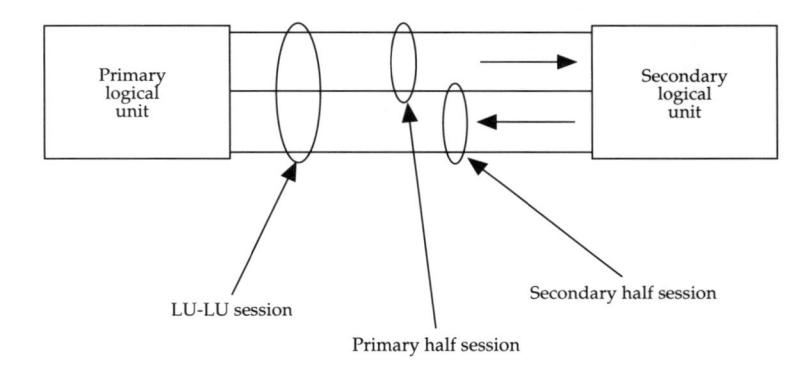

Figure 13   Half sessions

A **session** comprises two half sessions, one in each direction. So, an **LU-LU session** comprises two half sessions. One half session is from **primary LU** to **secondary LU** and the other is from secondary LU to primary LU (Fig. 13).

The direction from primary LU to secondary LU is called the primary half session. The direction from secondary LU to primary LU is called the secondary half session.

The main point of half sessions is that we can have different session parameters on each half session. If you analyse the **BIND command**, it can be seen that certain parameters are set for the half session, and some for the session. An example is given below.

Example of setting different parameters on two half sessions

Say we have an application where PCs communicate with a **mainframe** application. The **session type** is irrelevant here, but data is

Hierarchy

passed in both directions. Buffer space in the mainframe application is limited, and there is no significant restriction in PC buffer space.

We want to restrict the size of **RUs** from the PC to the host to something small, 128 bytes say. We do not want to significantly restrict the size of RUs from the host to the PC. However, we must specify a limit, so let us use 4096 bytes.

We would set the session parameters as follows:

- the maximum RU size sent by the primary half session is set to 4096 bytes
- the maximum RU size sent by the secondary half session is set to 128 bytes

Hierarchy

Here we have an NCP with three lines, one of which is multidrop. For a particular resource to be active, the resource immediately above it in the hierarchy must be active. The status of resources on the same level or below is irrelevant.

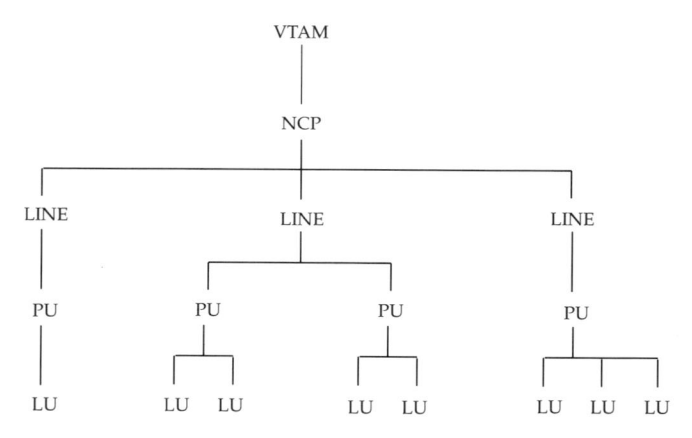

```
                           VTAM
                             |
                            NCP
          _____|_____
         |                   |                   |
        LINE                LINE                LINE
         |                   |                   |
         PU         _____|_____           PU
         |         |                  |         _|_____
         LU        PU                 PU        |       |
              ____|____           ____|____     PU      PU
             |         |         |         |   _|_    __|__
             LU        LU        LU        LU  | |   |  |  |
                                              LU LU  LU LU LU
```

Figure 14   3270 hierarchy for VTAM activation

SNA resources have a hierarchy for **activation** and inactivation (Fig. 14). It is not possible to successfully activate a resource unless the resource above it in the hierarchy is active.

If you think about this it is obvious. Active means 'in **session** with the **SSCP**', or the SSCP is talking to the resource. If the SSCP is not talking to resource A, then it will not be able to talk to resource B if B is attached to A.

The practical upshot of this is that **NCPs** must be active before lines must be active before **cluster controllers** must be active before terminals.

Host node

A host node is a **subarea node** which contains **VTAM**. Sometimes called a host subarea node, a host node is one of the two types of subarea node.

IND$FILE

IND$FILE is a **mainframe** utility designed for **file transfer** between PCs and mainframes. It runs under **TSO, CICS** and **VM**. Usually it is run under TSO from the command line or under ISPF.

IND$FILE is sometimes called IND£FILE on certain systems, which is just another name for the same product.

IND$FILE is designed to work with an IBM PC program called FTTERM. However, a number of manufacturers have written compatible PC software.

The system uses a **3270** structured field data stream and so uses a session type 2. This means it is not particularly efficient.

When sending data to the host, the system emulates a very fast typist filling up a 3270 screen, and then pressing the enter key. When receiving data from the host, the system emulates a very fast reader reading all the data on the screen, and then pressing enter for the next screen of data.

Using a 3270 interactive **session** to do **file transfer**, which can be considered to be a batch type operation, gives us a number of issues to consider:

1. *Circuit loading*. What is the effect on other interactive users when someone is doing file transfer?
2. *File transfer times*. The 3270 datastream is a comparatively inefficient tool for file transfer.
3. *Host loading*. What is the effect on the host of running file transfer at interactive priorities?

So why is it used? Because it is free. An application specially designed for file transfer will cost about £10 000.

The performance versus cost issues are complicated, as they affect every component in the system. A good rule of thumb is that IND$FILE is fine for low-volume applications or where mainframe resource is perceived to cost nothing. Otherwise it is worth considering an alternative to IND$FILE.

JES

JES stands for job entry subsystem. It is the software responsible for starting, stopping and allocating resources to batch jobs. JES2 and JES3 are both in use, although JES2 is most common. **VTAM** is started as a JES batch job as part of the **mainframe** IPL. So VTAM can be considered as a JES batch job in the same way as all the other system software.

However, when we are using JES to send data to network printers, then JES becomes a **VTAM application**. JES is defined to VTAM in the same way as ordinary online applications, and a definition for JES is placed in the VTAM libraries. The JES to VTAM **session** is normally started automatically.

The upshot of this is that from an operating system programmer's view, VTAM is a JES batch job. However, from a communications system programmer's view, JES is a VTAM application.

Jokes

If IBM had designed the telephone system, everybody in the world would have to hang up whenever a new phone was connected.

There is a little bit of truth in this. IBM systems still tend to be table driven, and the tables are only looked at when the system is started. So to put in a minor definition change to **VTAM**, for example, could result in the whole network being taken down.

However, it is now possible for some network definition changes to be done 'on the fly', and more systems are self-defining. The downside of this is that it will be more difficult to determine exactly how the network thinks it is defined, and self-generating systems will go spectacularly wrong when they do go wrong (to really screw things up properly you need a computer). Dummy definitions are usually added to table-driven systems and activated when necessary, and planning changes never hurt anyone.

Q: How many IBMers does it take to change a light bulb?

A: 100—one to change the bulb, and 99 to write the following manuals:

- DF32-2983/2 iridescent light source hardware planning
- SH23-6297/1 iridescent light source users' guide
- GH12-2341/5 iridescent light source problem determination

IBM manuals are plentiful, comprehensive and up to date. Just about everything you need to know about IBM systems is documented somewhere in great detail. The problem is first of all finding the information, and then understanding the language. There is no substitute for practice.

Layers

SNA is designed as a seven-layer **architecture**. Each layer has a specific function. Layers work in pairs, that is, the path control layer in a part of the network 'talks' to another path control layer via data **link** control. Each network component contains a subset of layers. It is important to remember that when data is traversing a network, it does not always pass down all the layers and then back up, but may pass up a number of layers only to go down again.

A good example of the value of the layering system was the addition of seven-colour support for 3270 terminals. This only required a change to the presentation services layer.

IBM defines the function of the layers as follows:

1. *Transaction services*: provides application services such as distributed database access and document interchange.
2. *Presentation services*: formats data for different presentation media and coordinates the sharing of resources.
3. *Data flow control*: synchronizes data flow and correlates exchanges of data and groups of related data into units.
4. *Transmission control*: paces data exchanges to match processing capacity and enciphers data if security is needed.
5. *Path control*: routes data between source and destination and controls data traffic in the network.
6. *Data link control*: transmits data between adjacent **nodes**.
7. *Physical control*: connects adjacent nodes physically and electrically.

Layers — an alternative view

The exact functionality of the various **layers** is unclear and confusing to say the least! The important points to remember are as follows:

- the layers exist
- **end users** enter the SNA network via **transaction** services

In practice, we rarely meet the layers in the real world. My advice is to forget about them until you are forced to find out more. However, you are unlikely to need to work with the layers again. This probably sounds heretical, but it is practical.

LEN end node

The LEN end node is the least functional of the three types of T2.1 node types.
The main functionality of the LEN end node is as follows:
1. CP-CP **sessions** are not supported.
2. The services of an adjacent **APPN network node** can be used, but all remote LUs must be pre-defined as if they exist on the adjacent network **node**. This means that the LEN end node is heavily dependent on the network node for connections within the network.

Links

Adjacent **nodes** are connected together by links. A link consists of the link connection, which is the physical medium of transmission (e.g. copper 4 wire and modems), and two or more **link stations**.

Link header

Link header	Information field	Link trailer

Figure 15   The link header

The link header (LH) is the string of bytes that is added on to the front of a lump of data in order to transmit it across a **link** (Fig. 15). In conjunction with the **link trailer**, the link header can be thought of as the link protocol.

The lump of data in this case is usually referred to as the information field or I-field. The precise word is **BTU**, but this is rarely used.

The **SDLC** LH is 3 bytes long; the **X25** LH is 6 bytes long; and the **token ring** LH is a minimum of 15 bytes as it has various optional fields.

See also the sections on the **link trailer** and **units of data**.

Link stations

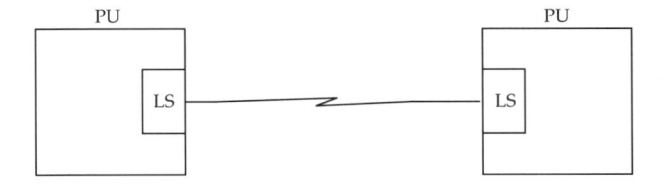

Figure 16 Link stations

Link stations (LS) attach SNA **nodes** to **links** (Fig. 16). They comprise hardware that provides the link connection and software that runs the data link protocol. For example, to attach a 3745 to an **SDLC** link with a V24 interface requires the correct interface hardware, and some software that can 'talk' SDLC.

Network messages and manuals that use the term link station can sometimes be referring to the opposite end of the link. In this case, the link station can be thought of as a representation of the PU at the distant end of the link. The link stations referred to when an **NCP** is displayed refer to other PUs.

Link trailer

The link trailer (LT) is the string of bytes that is added on to the end of a lump of data in order to transmit it across a **link**. The link trailer includes a **frame** check sequence that is used to check whether the data has been corrupted during transmission.

The **SDLC** LT is 3 bytes long; the **X25** LT is 3 bytes long; and the **token ring** LT is 6 bytes long.

See also the sections on the **link header** and **units of data**.

Local address

The local address is used within a **cluster controller** to refer to a particular **logical unit** (LU), or to the **physical unit** (PU) itself (Fig. 17). The local address is translated to and from the **network address** by the **boundary function** which is typically **NCP** or **VTAM**. The local address is used almost exclusively in the context of **3270** control units.

Logical units

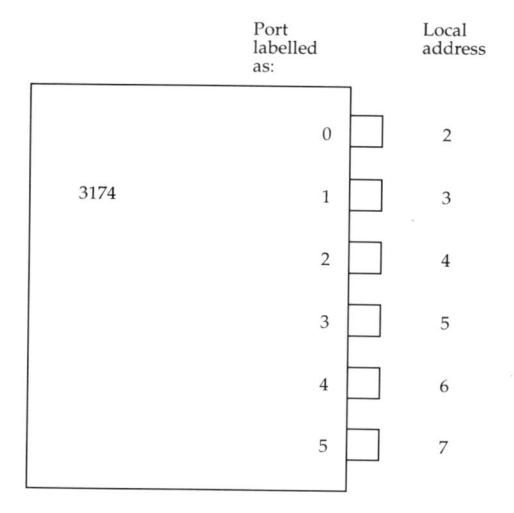

```
                    Port          Local
                    labelled      address
                    as:

                      0  ☐         2

          3174        1  ☐         3

                      2  ☐         4

                      3  ☐         5

                      4  ☐         6

                      5  ☐         7
```

Figure 17   Cluster controller local addressing

The local address is located in the following places:

- the **transmission header** in a PU2 datastream
- the NCP or VTAM definition for the PU
- the 3174 configuration files

Local address settings are as follows:

- 00 always refers to the PU itself
- 01 is never used when referring to the cluster controller
- 02 refers to the first LU on the cluster controller
- 03 refers to the second LU on the cluster controller
- 04 refers to the third LU on the cluster controller

This can get confusing, as on a 3174 the first terminal port is marked as number 0. VTAM terminal naming conventions should also take this potential confusion into account.

Logical units

Every **end user** has an SNA thing that lets it into the network. This 'thing' is called a logical unit or **LU**.

The LUs manage the flow of data across the network on behalf of the end users. The point of this is that the end users do not have to become involved in communications. Data is passed to the LU and the end user waits for confirmation that it has been delivered.

Logical unit types 31

The number of end users that can be supported by a single LU depends on the implementation of the LU and end user. For example, **TSO** uses an LU for each end user, while **CICS** supports multiple end users on a single LU. Terminal systems typically have one LU per end user.

The point where the end user stops and the LU starts can be very difficult to determine. However, we do not need to worry about this question. The important thing is how many LUs are required, and where they are. This is usually easy to determine.

Logical unit types

LUs are classified into LU types depending on the subset of SNA functionality that they implement. Different **end users** require different subsets of SNA functionality to gain access to the SNA network. Thus the LU type required depends on the end user that is to be supported.

SNA defines the following types of **logical unit**. The definition describes the end user to end user connection that is to be supported.

LU0

Any combination of SNA LU definitions that is valid. This is defined by the user for specific applications.

LU1

Used for application program to character oriented devices such as printers or terminals without screen **addressing**. This LU type is used to support asynchronous terminals via **X25** among other things.

LU2

Used for application program to interactive **3270** terminal.

LU3

Used for application program to printer using the 3270 data stream.

LU4

Used for application program to intelligent terminal. This is most often used in office automation.

LU6.1

Used for application program to application program.

LU6.2

Used for application program to application program. Similar to **LU6.1**, but with additional features. This is the only LU type defined for **SAA**.

LU7

Used for application program to interactive **5250** terminal.

The most common LU types, are 1, 2, 6.2 and 7. The LU type of a particular LU can change during its lifetime. For example, it is possible for an intelligent device to accept both LU2 data (interactive 3270) and then LU1 data (printing). The data could be treated differently: LU2 data put on the screen, and LU1 data sent to an auxiliary printer. This is not a common feature on IBM manufactured equipment, but is implemented by a number of other manufacturers.

The phrase '**session type**' is also used to describe the end users in an **LU-LU session**.

Logmodes

The logmode, or logon mode, is a set of **VTAM** parameters that is used to set the session parameters in the **BIND command** for a particular **LU-LU session**. Logmodes are grouped together and placed in VTAM tables called logmode tables.

The logmode to be used is specified when the **request** for an LU-LU session is made. This can be done explicitly, by specifying the logmode to be used in the logon request, or can be allowed to default. See also the section on **USS tables**. Be careful, however, as the logmode requested can sometimes be modified or even ignored by the system, resulting in a BIND image completely different from what you expected. If there is any doubt as to the contents of the BIND, do not rely on looking at the logmode tables, take a trace.

Loose talk

In order to be able to know exactly what you are talking about the correct words have to be used. This is especially true in SNA. The trouble is that certain people tend to use the wrong words. This can be for one of two reasons—either they are being lazy or they do not know what they are talking about. The trick is to decide which category the person is in. However, there are a number of words that most people, competent or not, tend to use incorrectly, but because everybody knows what they are talking about everybody understands.

Example 1: NCP 3745 or PU4

If we want to be perfectly precise about it, **NCP** is the software that runs in the hardware that is the 3745 communications controller: together they perform the function of a PU4. If we use NCP when we are talking about a piece of hardware people usually know what we are talking about. For example, to say that additional memory is required in an NCP is technically incorrect, although it is the sort of phrase that is often used without confusion.

Example 2: frames

When a lump of data is moved from an application program to a terminal, it undergoes various transformations. At each point the data is in a specific format and has an equally specific acronym. For example, **logical units** read and write **RUs** while data transmitted across a **link** is properly referred to as a **BTU**. It is common practice to refer to any particular lump of data as a '**frame**'—the use of the word 'frame' in place of BTU is becoming common, and is also used by IBM. However, if dataflow is being discussed and people refer to a frame, it is often very useful to determine exactly what they are talking about.

LU-LU sessions

LU-LU sessions are the most important **sessions** in a network. They represent real people doing real work, which justifies the existence of the network, and provides us with jobs.

LU-LU sessions are activated, by definition, by the **BIND command**. The **primary LU** sends the BIND, and the **secondary LU** receives the BIND. The session is only considered to be **active** when a positive BIND response has been sent by the SLU and received by the PLU.

The usual way for an LU-LU session to commence is for a terminal user to send a LOGON message to the **SSCP**, requesting a session with a particular application. The **sequence** of commands is illustrated in Appendix B. Another way to start a session is for an application to **request** a session with a terminal, for example in printing; or the SSCP can force a session to start between an application and a terminal.

A common method is to use an application called a **network solicitor**. All terminal LUs are forced into session with this application, which then controls session setup with other applications.

LU6.2

The principle of LU6.2 is very straightforward. It is an LU specified for application program to application program communication. The important point is that the application program does not necessarily have to reside in a host **mainframe**. It could reside, and often does, in an **AS/400** system or a PC, or even in something that looks like a terminal. This means that the **logical unit type** is independent of the system that is using the network. For example, LU6.2 can be used to carry either 3270 sessions or for **file transfer** that would traditionally be carried in an LU1 data stream.

LU6.2 is the only LU type specified for use with **SAA**. This means that as SAA systems become more common, so will LU6.2. At the moment, LU6.2 is mainly used in LANs and for certain specialized applications.

Unlike conventional LUs, LU6.2 can operate on a **peer-to-peer** basis. This can be contrasted with the master-slave relationship in an LU2 session. In certain circumstances LU6.2 does not require an LU-**SSCP** session to function. This is known as LU-SSCP independence or independent LUs.

The reason LU6.2 is important is that it provides the flexibility required for the more advanced communications functions that will be required in the future. The other LU types are all significantly limited, but not LU6.2.

Mainframes

Mainframes are important in SNA because of the traditionally hierarchical nature of SNA systems. This will continue to be so for some time. From a networking point of view, the only issue of importance is whether a mainframe contains an **SSCP**, i.e. is it running **VTAM**? Current mainframe technology means that it is possible to run more than one operating system on a single box. It is also possible to run a single operating system on multiple CPUs. From a networking point of view, the number of mainframes equals the number of VTAMs. For example, we have a single CPU that runs **VM** with VTAM and two MVS systems, each with VTAM. As we have three VTAMs in the system from a networking standpoint we will consider this one CPU to be three mainframes.

Mainframe structure

Figures 18, 19 and 20 illustrate the more important aspects of mainframe structure from a communications point of view.

Figure 18 illustrates the physical connections between a **mainframe** and a **3270** terminal. An important point is that the **link** connection between the **FEP** and **cluster controller** is the slowest part of the system by a long way. In most systems, the delay due to the **channel** and coaxial cable can be ignored for performance analysis calculations.

Figure 19 on page 36 illustrates the most common ways of connecting different SNA devices together.

Box a is a 3174 that is channel-attached to the mainframe. This gives a high speed and high capacity connection, and is usually used when the 3174 is in the same building as the mainframe. Multiple 3174s can be daisy-chained on a single channel.

Box b is a standard channel-attached 3745. It is also connected to

Mainframe

Channel connection. Speed a minimum of several megabits per second. Shared with other peripherals.

Front end processor

Link connection, usually over PTT circuit. Only shared in the case of multidrop. Speed from 4800 to 64k bits per second.

Cluster controller

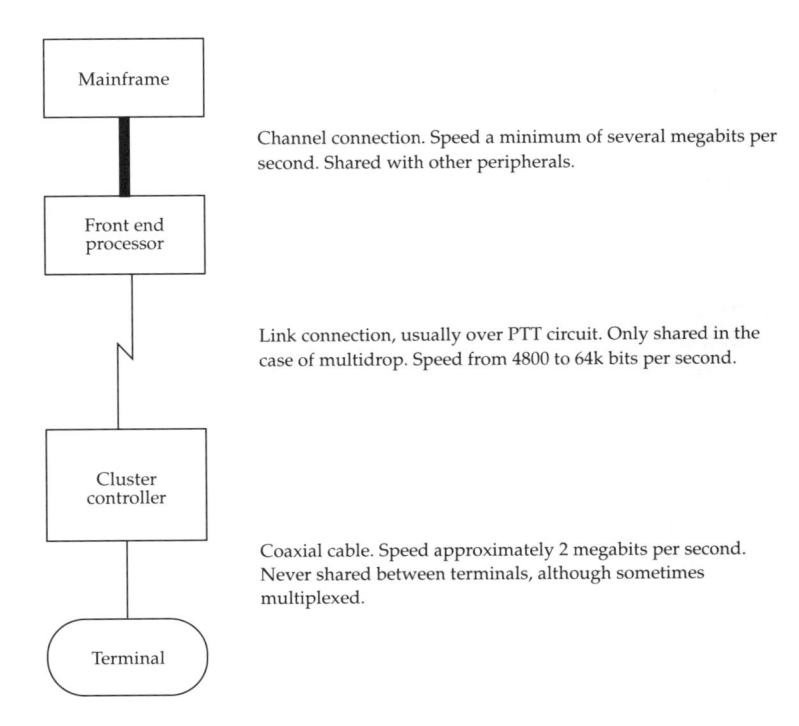

Coaxial cable. Speed approximately 2 megabits per second. Never shared between terminals, although sometimes multiplexed.

Terminal

Figure 18   Mainframe links and typical speeds

Mainframe structure

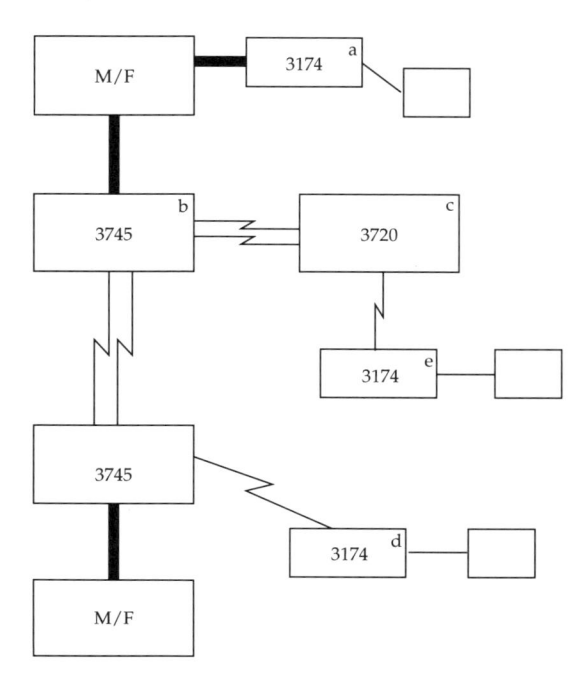

Figure 19 S/370 system structure

another 3745 via multiple links. This gives us a physical data path between the two mainframes. It is also possible to channel-connect the two mainframes together directly. The considerations for channel versus link connecting mainframes are fairly straightforward speed, throughput and cost issues.

Box c is a **3720** communications controller link-attached to a 3745. It is acting as a concentrator for 3174 **cluster controllers**. The most

Operating system (MVS)					
Telecommunications access method (VTAM)				Job entry subsystem (JES)	
Appl. A (CICS)	Appl. B (CICS)	Appl. C (TSO)	Netview	Batch Job A	Batch Job B
User-written applications		ISPF			

Figure 20 Mainframe overview

common reason for implementing this configuration is to save PTT circuit costs and provide additional integrity.

Box d is a link-attached 3174. This is the most common way of attaching a cluster controller to a mainframe system.

Box e is a link-attached 3174.

Figure 20 illustrates the hierarchy of the mainframe system from the point of view of the operating system.

Major node

The major node is a concept applicable to **VTAM** systems. A major node is a group of **minor nodes**. In most systems, the minor nodes are grouped together into major nodes in a logical fashion. For example, cross-domain resources relating to a particular distant system would be grouped into a single cross-domain resource major node. Each major node definition is put into its own member in SYS1.VTAMLST. The **node hierarchy** operates for major nodes and minor nodes. It is possible to do a VTAM display of major nodes by using the D NET,MAJNODES commands.

Minor node

A minor node is an individual **VTAM** resource—for example, the definition of a particular application LU or a particular cross-domain resource manager. Minor nodes can be displayed using the VTAM D NET,ID=xxxxx command.

MSNF

MSNF stands for multi system networking facility. It is the **VTAM** feature that gives the capability of **cross-domain networking**.

NAU

NAU stands for network addressable unit. An NAU is an element in the network that has a unique address. In practice an NAU is either an LU, a PU or an **SSCP**.

The address of the NAU is referred to as the **network address**. The network address is unique within the network, and is used to route data between NAUs.

NCCF

NCCF stands for network communications control facility. It is the forerunner to **netview**, with basically the same functionality as the **netview command facility**.

NCCF is a **3270** application that is used to facilitate network operations.

When NCCF is running, and an NCCF operator is logged on, all **VTAM** messages go to the NCCF screen. **VTAM commands** can be entered by the NCCF operator. Thus the network operations load is completely separate from the system console.

NCCF has other features to assist in network operations. Logging all activity to disk, timed execution of commands, simplification of VTAM commands and command lists are a few examples.

NCCF is much less common than netview.

Please refer to the sections on netview and the netview command facility.

NCP

NCP stands for network control program. It is the software that runs in the IBM range of 37xx communications controllers. NCP is downline loaded by **VTAM** into the 37xx, its communications controller, either across a channel or across a link.

The process by which NCPs are built is known as NCP generation. The systems programmer builds a data set that describes the communications controller hardware and the configuration of the lines, **cluster controllers** and terminals that attach to it. This data set is used as input to an IBM-supplied generation program. This program builds the object code, which is loaded into the communications controller. The object code is a special assembler, similar to S\370 assembler but specific to the IBM communications controllers.

Some IBM-compatible communications controllers will run NCP and others will not.

This data set is also placed in SYS1.VTAMLST, or equivalent, and will be the NCP **major node** definition.

Netview

Netview is IBM's strategic network management system.

Netview is currently a **VTAM 3270** application, although it will in the future run on other hardware platforms—**AS/400** will be the first.

It is virtually impossible to run an SNA network effectively without netview. Most installations use it, or some equivalent.

The structure of the netview application is similar to that of **TSO**. Thus there is a main task, and various user subtasks. Subsets of subtasks provide the following features:

- Netview command facility
- Netview hardware monitor
- Netview performance monitor
- Netview session monitor
- Netview status monitor

Each of the above is discussed in the following sections.

Netview is an extremely important part of IBM's strategic networking direction. It is undergoing constant development and this will no doubt continue. Netview will remain an important and useful network management tool.

Netview command facility

The netview command facility allows the netview operator to enter **netview** and **VTAM commands** and receive netview and VTAM messages. Other features, such as command lists and timer commands, make the netview command facility a powerful network operator's tool.

Netview command facility is sometimes referred to as **NCCF**.

Netview compatibility

Although most people have heard of it, it can be argued that there is no such thing as netview compatibility. The phrase itself has the obvious meaning of being compatible with the netview family of products. However, as netview is being continually upgraded to support additional functionality there are very few products on the market that can support every one of netview's features.

The way to address the issue of netview compatibility is to consider which of the particular netview features are required in a particular system, for example, the ability to support **response time** monitor or the ability to support vital product data information.

Netview hardware monitor

The netview hardware monitor is part of the **netview** suite of products. It is designed to store and process network errors and aid problem determination.

Network error information is stored on a database for later retrieval by the network operator. Each error has an explanation associated with it, including probable cause and recommended action. Certain types of error will be flagged immediately to the network operator as, for example, when a transient error threshold is exceeded.

The netview hardware monitor is sometimes referred to as **NPDA**.

Netview performance monitor

The netview performance monitor (NPM) is part of the **netview** suite of products. It is designed to produce statistics on the loading and performance of various network components. There are two parts to NPM: the NPM netview application and some NPM code that must be added to **NCP**.

The netview application stores the performance data and handles the online operator interface to allow an NPM operator to access the data and receive performance alerts as necessary. It also allows the operator to display **RTM** data.

The NPM code added to NCP performs functions such as measuring line utilization and counting re-transmissions. This data is then passed back to netview.

Netview session monitor

The netview session monitor is part of the **netview** suite of products. It is designed to gather information on **sessions** and present it to the netview operator.

Session monitor gathers **RTM** data from the network which is processed by **netview performance monitor**.

Netview status monitor

The netview status monitor is part of the **netview** suite of programs. It provides the netview operator with a global picture of the status of

Network address

all the resources in the network. In addition, it allows the operator to activate and deactivate resources without the need to enter commands. This is done using cursor positioning or a light pen.

Network address

The network address uniquely identifies a particular resource in a network. It consists of two parts, the **subarea** to which the resource belongs, and the element number within that subarea. The two parts are called the subarea address field, and the element address field respectively.

The element number can be calculated by counting up the resources in the subarea until the required resource is reached (Fig. 21). A simpler and more practical way is to take a trace of the resource, and look at the network address.

The network address can have two formats:

1. *The 16 bit network address*: the network address is 16 bits long. The number of bits used for the subarea address field is hard

Here, we have an NCP with two lines. One has two 3174s multidropped, and the other has a single 3174. The element addresses for each resource are given in large type. We simply number the resources in order.

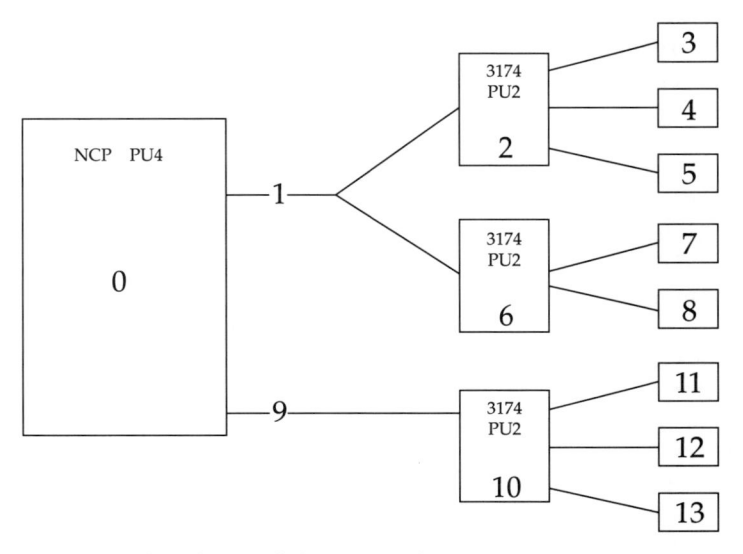

Figure 21 Calculation of element number

coded into the network definitions. Different networks will have different lengths set for the subarea and element address fields.

2. *The extended 23 bit network address*: the network address is 24 (sic) bits long. Bits 0–7 are used for the subarea address field, and bits 9–23 are used for the element address field.

All subareas in the network use the same method of analysing the network address.

The extended 23 bit network address is a comparatively recent enhancement to overcome the following problems with the 16 bit network address.

The limit on the length of the address fields imposed a limit on the number of subareas and the number of elements within each subarea.

Example

Say we have 50 subareas in a network.

The length of the subarea address field would have to be 6 bits. 50 = binary 110010

We have, therefore, 10 bits for the element address field 16-6.

With 10 binary bits, we can address up to 1023 ($2^{**}10$ -1). We therefore have a maximum of 1023 elements per subarea.

If we are running 3174 **cluster controllers** with 32 terminals, we will use 34 elements per cluster controller (one for the line, one for the PU and one for each of the terminals). Therefore, we have a maximum of 30 (1023/34) lines on an **FEP**.

Every **node** in the network had to use the same lengths for the subarea and element address fields. This tended to cause problems when connecting two different networks together.

Example—a 16 bit network address

Say the network is defined such that bits 0-4 of the network address are used for the subarea element field. The subarea address field of a particular resource is 5. The element address field of a particular resource is 513. What is the network address?

For the subarea address field: the subarea address is 5, which is binary 101 (3 bits). We must use 5 bits for the subarea address field. Therefore, the subarea address field is binary 00101.

For the element address field: the element address is 513 which is binary 1000000001 (10 bits). We have used 5 bits from a total of 16 for the subarea address field. Therefore, we must use 11 (16-5) bits for the element address field. Therefore, the element address field is 01000000001.

Network management

The network address is the subarea address field followed by the element address field, that is:

0010101000000001

To convert to hex, we must group the binary digits into groups of four thus:

0010 1010 0000 0001

This is 2A 01 in hex.

So the network 16 bit network address of the resource will appear as hex 2A 01 on a trace. In this example, the subarea number seems to have disappeared completely.

Example—a 16 bit network address

Say the network is defined such that bits 0–5 of the network address are used for the subarea element field. The network address is 0001001001100001. What are the subarea and element addresses?

First we must break the network address down into subarea address fields and element address fields.

Bits 0–5 (6 bits) of the network address are used for the subarea element field, so we divide the network address thus:

000100 1001100001

The subarea address is binary 000100, i.e. decimal 4. The element address is binary 1001100001, i.e. decimal 609.

Network management

Network management has very little to do with expensive network management hardware and software and everything to do with getting your act together! There is no point in getting a clever datascope, if the people who are operating it do not understand the protocol that is being used. Similarly, it can be argued that a high-powered PC-based network management system is useless, if the network operators do not know exactly when each particular service should be available.

Network management can be loosely divided into three parts:

- agreeing in detail with the user exactly what service will be delivered
- delivering what was agreed
- telling the user that what was agreed has in fact been achieved

Network solicitors

The complexity of the network management task will depend on the size of the network and the network users' requirements. However, no matter how small the network, if any one of the three above steps is not completed the result will be unhappy users.

Network solicitors

The standard method of logging on to an interactive application on a **mainframe**-based system is not particularly user-friendly even with customized **USS tables** and **USS messages**. Network solicitors are **VTAM applications** that are designed to make the process of logging on to an application easier for the user.

Typically, a terminal LU is forced into **session** with the network solicitor as soon as it is powered up. A screen of data is then displayed informing the terminal user what applications are available, and what keystrokes to use to log on. Often password security is implemented on the network solicitor, saving the user from multiple password entries when multiple applications are accessed.

Network solicitors usually have a multiple session feature, where the terminal user can access multiple applications without having to

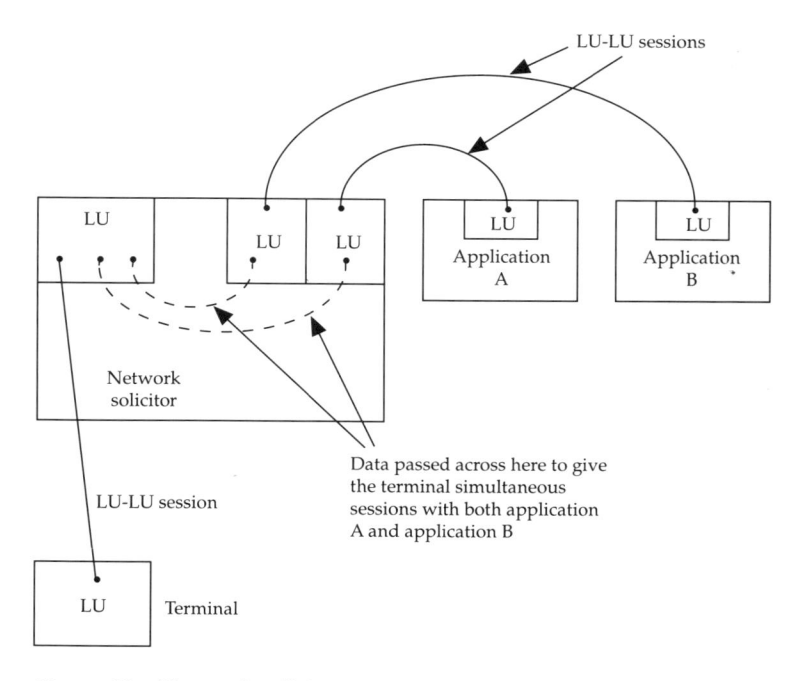

Figure 22   Network solicitor structure

Node

log off and back on again. Switching between sessions is usually by hot key. This is commonly achieved by the network solicitor having multiple LUs for a single user terminal. One LU is used to communicate with the terminal. The others effectively look like terminals, and so can 'log on' to applications. Data is passed from an application to an LU in the network solicitor. It is then passed to the LU used to communicate with the terminal and then sent to the terminal. Figure 22 illustrates this.

NJE

NJE stands for network job entry. NJE is **JES** to JES data transfer using **MSNF**.

The mechanism is to set up a JES to JES **session**. The two JESs are then talking and so can pass data.

Node

A node is hardware plus software that implements the **layers** defined by SNA. There are two types of nodes:

- **subarea nodes**
- **peripheral nodes**

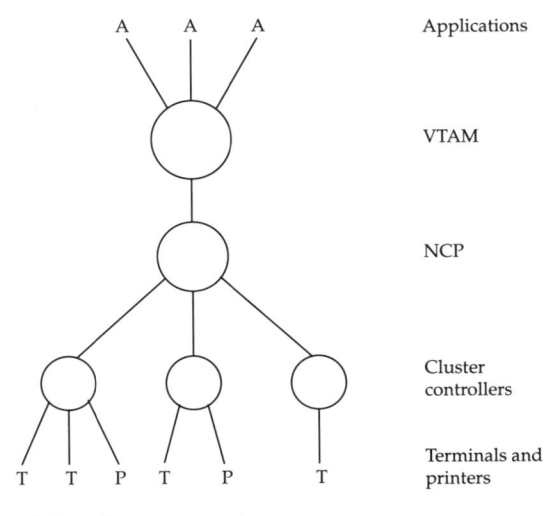

All the circles represent nodes.

Figure 23 Node definition

Subarea nodes can be broken down further:

- **host nodes**
- **communication controller nodes**

This definition is architecturally correct, but difficult to understand. A more usable definition, illustrated in Fig. 23, is akin to the mathematical definition of a node.

NPA

NPA stands for network performance analyser. It is the old version of **netview performance monitor**.

Please refer to the section on the netview performance monitor for information on NPA functionality.

NPDA

NPDA stands for network problem determination application. It is the old version of the **netview hardware monitor**.

Please refer to the section on the netview hardware monitor for information on NPDA functionality.

NPSI

NPSI stands for NCP packet switching interface.

In order to support **X25** directly on the **FEP**, an additional piece of software is required, running under **NCP**. This piece of software is called NPSI (Fig. 24).

NPSI effectively fools the NCP into thinking an IBM device that talks **SDLC** is attached. This is a typical method of attaching a non-SNA device.

NPSI supports LAP or LAPB protocols. Each X25 circuit into the FEP can support multiple logical groups, each with multiple logical **channels**. Each logical channel equates to what would have been an SDLC circuit had SDLC been used (Fig. 25).

There are many functions and features available in NPSI to support and control terminal **sessions**. The two most common are **QLLC**, which is used to support SNA devices, and XXX, which is used to support asynchronous TTY devices.

See also the section entitled **SDLC or X25?**

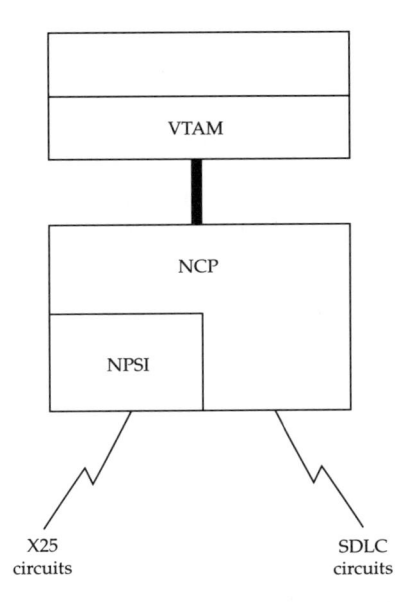

Figure 24   NPSI location and basic functionality

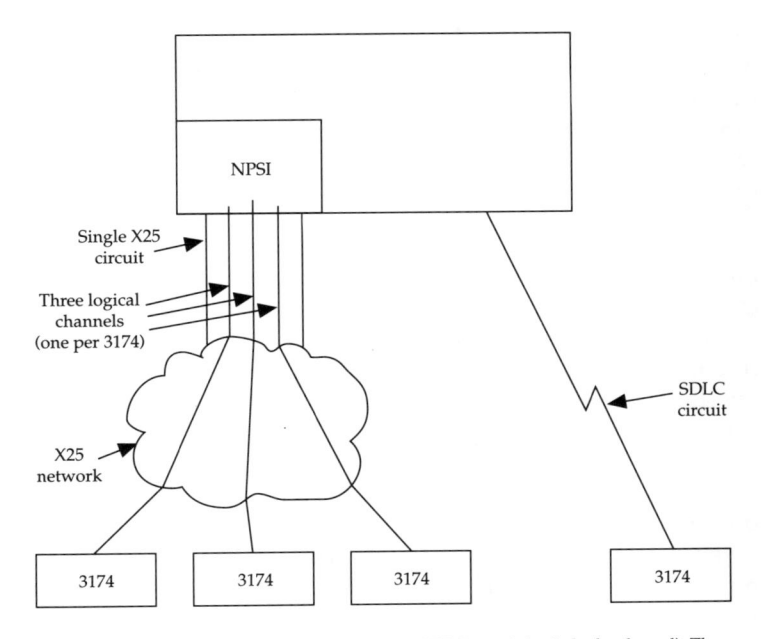

Each logical channel (SVC or PVC) equates to an SDLC circuit (switched or leased). The SNA functionality of all four 3174s is the same. SNA functionality is independent of circuit protocol.

Figure 25   Using NPSI to support 3174s

NPSI overhead

There is a lot of misleading information concerning NPSI overhead. Let us, firstly, define exactly what we are discussing. Consider the **NCP** resources required to support a particular terminal population and traffic pattern using **SDLC**. We should include 37XX CPU cycles, 37XX buffer requirements and circuit capacity. If we use **X25** via NPSI instead of SDLC, different amounts of resource will be required. With NPSI the difference is usually more, and this is called the NPSI overhead.

CPU cycles

The data must be processed twice, firstly by NCP and then by NPSI. This means that extra CPU cycles are consumed.

NCP buffers

Data is buffered twice—once in NPSI and again in NCP, so extra storage will be required. However, the NPSI code takes up 37XX buffer space, so there will also be less buffers available.

Circuit capacity

The **X25** frame header is 6 bytes, compared to the 3 byte SDLC header. Also, it is common for multiple X25 **frames** to be used for a transmission that would be transmitted in a single SDLC **BLU**. Thus more circuit capacity is required. However, X25 will run full duplex, which is not always possible with SDLC. This may reduce the circuit capacity required.

NPSI imposes a significant overhead on the NCP compared to native SDLC. However, this is not necessarily a problem. What is critical is whether the extra resources are available. For example, it does not matter if NPSI will increase CPU utilization by 100 per cent, if current utilization is only 10 per cent. Whether a particular overhead is important will depend on the installation.

Calculation of the various overheads is a complicated exercise. A useful rule of thumb is that the NPSI overhead is between 5 per cent and 10 per cent. So if our current system is SDLC, and the maximum buffer utilization is 100 buffers, changing to X25 everywhere will give a maximum utilization in the order of 110 buffers. Do not forget, however, that the buffer pool will be reduced. The point is that if you are faced with someone who is talking about a 30 per cent overhead, ask where the figures come from. This discussion also applies to the **AS/400** and **S/3X** systems. In these cases, NPSI is not used, but the principles remain the same.

NRZ and NRZI

1 0 1 1 0 0 1   Encoded using NRZ

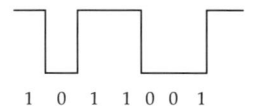

1 0 1 1 0 0 1

1 0 1 1 0 0 1   Encoded using NRZI if state is initially high

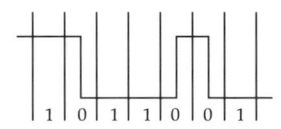

| 1 | 0 | 1 | 1 | 0 | 0 | 1 |

Figure 26   Example of NRZ and NRZI encoding

NRZ stands for non return to zero, and NRZI for non return to zero inverted. The two acronyms refer to the method of encoding used on the **SDLC** circuit (Fig. 26).

1. NRZ. Here, the transmitter uses a high state to indicate a 1 bit, and a low state to indicate a 0 bit.
2. NRZI. Here, the transmitter holds the same state to indicate a binary 1, and changes the state to indicate a binary 0.

NRZI is important in transmission systems that are sensitive to an unchanging state, or to a continually changing state. However, very few modern transmission systems are sensitive, so the setting has lost most of its significance. The standard in most installations is historical.

It is important that both primary and secondary ends of the SDLC link are set the same, otherwise there will be no communication.

NRZ or NRZI is set in the **NCP** line macro. NRZI=yes or NRZI=no is specified. It is one of those parameters that no one can remember how it was set.

NTO

NTO stands for network terminal option. It is an additional piece of code to **NCP** that allows for the connection of asynchronous and

50   Pacing

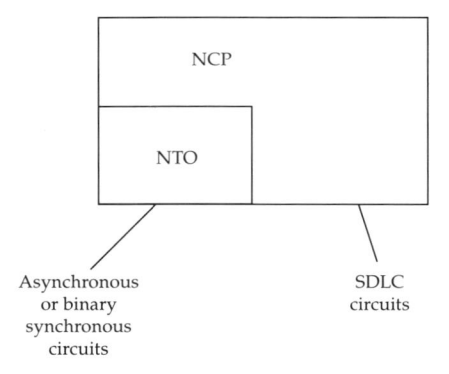

Figure 27   NTO location and basic functionality

certain BSC devices to NCP. The devices appear as **SDLC** 3767 terminals (Fig. 27).

As NTO is additional to NCP, it increases the buffers required and uses additional NCP cycles.

The major problem with NTO is that it requires one 37XX port per terminal. This is an expensive option, as 37XX ports are a comparatively expensive resource.

NTO is becoming less common now. The preferred options for many installations are either to use **NPSI**, not to support non-SNA terminals or to use a protocol converter of some kind.

Pacing

Pacing is the SNA mechanism that controls the rate at which data is moved around the network (Fig. 28).

In any network, certain components will be able to process received data faster than other components. If a fast component was sending data to a slow component, then the slow one would quickly become overloaded. The purpose of pacing is to ensure that network components are not overloaded, but at the same time maximize data throughput.

Two types of pacing are implemented in SNA networks. **Session level pacing**, which manages the flow of messages between LUs, and **virtual route pacing**, which manages the flow of messages between the two end **subareas** of a **virtual route**. Session level pacing controls the flow of **RUs**, and virtual route pacing controls the flow of **PIUs**.

The principle of pacing is that only a certain number of messages are transmitted at any one time. The system then waits for a pacing

Pacing

response, which indicates that more messages may be sent. Pacing definitions are as follows:

1. The pacing group is a group of messages that can be sent at one time.
2. The pacing window size is the number of messages contained in the pacing group.
3. The pacing response indicates that another pacing group can be sent.

This example uses an application program sending data to a printer. The printer is comparatively slow, but has a large buffer. As the two ends in this example are LUs, we are performing session level pacing. The pacing window size is 4.

```
Application              Printer                 Actions

        RU 1
        ─────────────►
        RU 2
        ─────────────►
        RU 3
        ─────────────►
        RU 4
        ─────────────►
                                    The pacing group has been sent, so the
                                    application must wait for a pacing response.
                                    As the printer has sufficient buffer space for
                                    another pacing group, it sends the pacing
        Pacing response             response.
        ◄─────────────
        RU 5
        ─────────────►
        RU 6
        ─────────────►
        RU 7
        ─────────────►
        RU 8
        ─────────────►
                                    The printer buffers cannot accommodate
                                    another pacing group. The printer withholds
                                    a pacing response until it has printed
                                    enough data for sufficient buffer space to
                                    become available.
        Pacing response
        ◄─────────────
             etc.
```

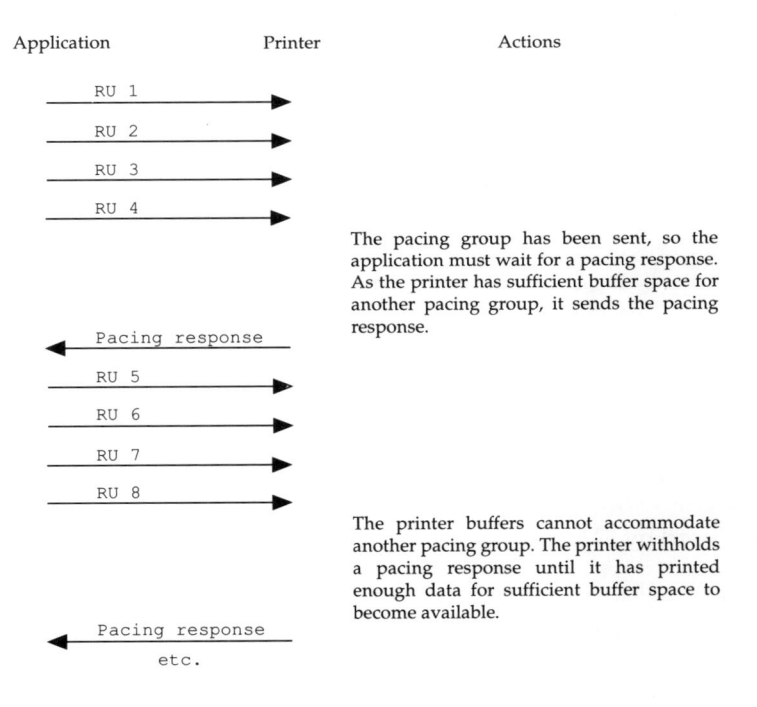

Figure 28   Simplified example of pacing

Parallel LU-LU sessions

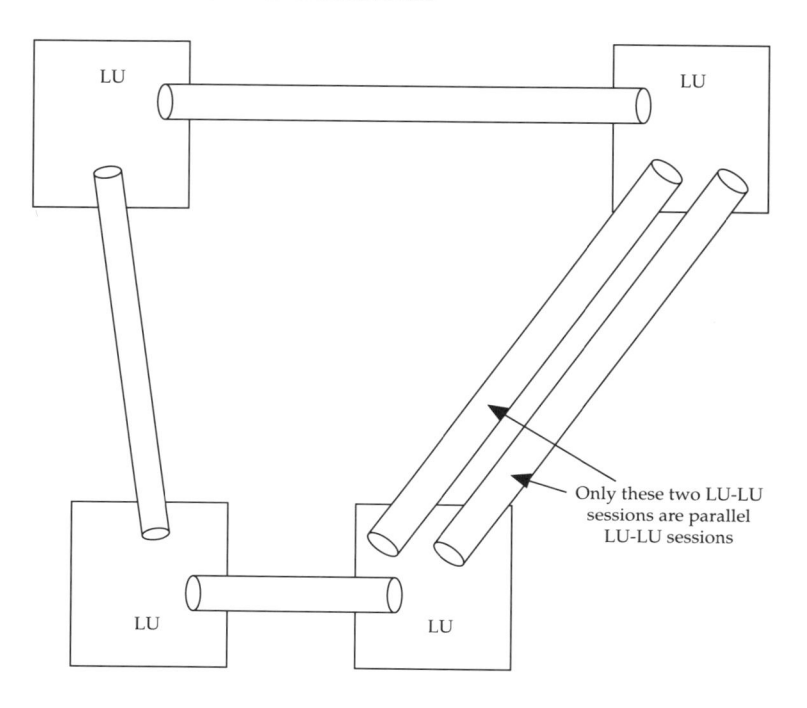

Figure 29 Parallel LU-LU sessions

(Only these two LU-LU sessions are parallel LU-LU sessions)

Parallel LU-LU sessions are multiple **LU-LU sessions** between the same two LUs at the same time (Fig. 29). They are most commonly used by **LU6.2**.

Peer-to-peer

Peer-to-peer is an IBM term that means that either system is able to activate a **session**. This can be contrasted with 'hierarchical' which means that only certain LUs are able to activate a session. Peer is often used instead of peer-to-peer.

PEP

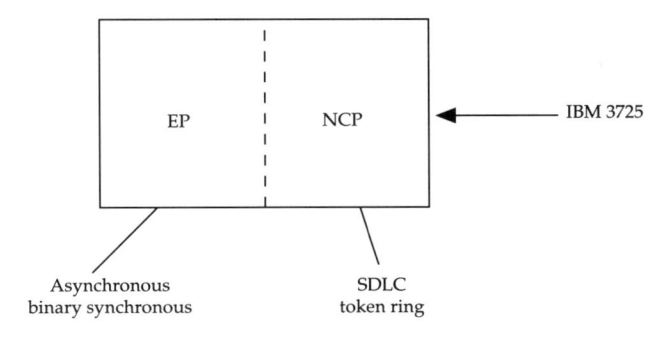

```
                    |
                    |
         EP         |    NCP    ◄────── IBM 3725
                    |
                    |
        /                   \
  Asynchronous           SDLC
  binary synchronous     token ring
```

Figure 30   Example of PEP

PEP stands for partitioned emulation program (Fig. 30). With PEP, the **NCP** is split into two logical sections. One of these sections can now be used to run non-SNA code, typically a program called EP (emulation program). This system is the most common way of running non-SNA protocols such as asynchronous and binary synchronous on an IBM **FEP**. It is becoming less common now.

Performance problems

This section is included for those who are unfamiliar with how to deal with performance problems. It is by no means comprehensive, but is intended to give some hints to newcomers. There are various performance monitoring tools available today, but we concentrate here on what needs to be done, rather than how to do it.

The difficulty with performance problems is defining exactly what the problem is, and how bad it is. The key to a solution is to use numbers to define what is going on. A problem will usually manifest itself with a user complaint along the lines of 'Every afternoon for the past few days, **response time** has been awful'. This sort of statement gives us no useful information on the problem, only that there is a problem. The sort of information required is:

> What is the user's definition of response time?
> What is the required response time? A number of seconds is required as an answer.
> When is the response bad? Dates and times required.
> When did the problem start? Date and time.

Who is affected, who is not affected?

What often happens is that the historical information is unsuitable for solving the problem. In that case some response time measurements must be taken to collect some base data. There are tools available to collect response time information, but often standing over a user with a stopwatch is the best way of assessing a performance problem. This has the added advantage that you are seen to be doing something, and the user is forced to define the problem in numbers. The effect of any changes on the system can then be determined by taking further measurements. Do not forget to change one thing at a time.

Peripheral nodes

Peripheral nodes are PUs that are not **subarea nodes**. This means that PU1, PU2 and **PU2.1** are all peripheral nodes. They usually attach to a subarea node and require support from a **boundary function**. Peripheral nodes use the **local address** to make routeing decisions.

Physical units

All networks need something to perform control functions. In SNA networks these 'things' are called physical units (PUs). A physical unit is control software, hardware or a combination of both.

A physical unit resides in every SNA node, and every **node** contains a physical unit. You may find it an interesting exercise to contemplate why IBM uses two different terms for what seems to be the same thing.

In spite of the name, it is not always possible to physically kick a physical unit, even though you may want to.

A special PU has overall control of a **mainframe** plus all the resources it controls. This PU is called the system services control point **(SSCP)**. Physical unit types are outlined below:

1. PU1: PU that supports multiple terminal LUs. The PU1 supports LU1, LU4 and LU7. The most common use for PU1 today is in the **S/3X** and **AS/400** range.
2. PU2: PU that supports multiple LU1s, LU2s, LU3s or **LU6.2s**. The 3174 is an example of a PU2. The PU2 must talk to a PU4 or a PU5.
3. PU2.1: Node type 2.1, as it should be called, is the PU type defined for **SAA**. It supports all LU types, but is designed to

Printing

work very closely with LU6.2. It also has sophisticated networking capabilities.
4. **PU4**: Functions as a communications controller, e.g. a 3745 running **NCP**.
5. **PU5**: This must contain an **SSCP**. For practical purposes PU5 and SSCP can usually be taken to mean the same thing.

PIU

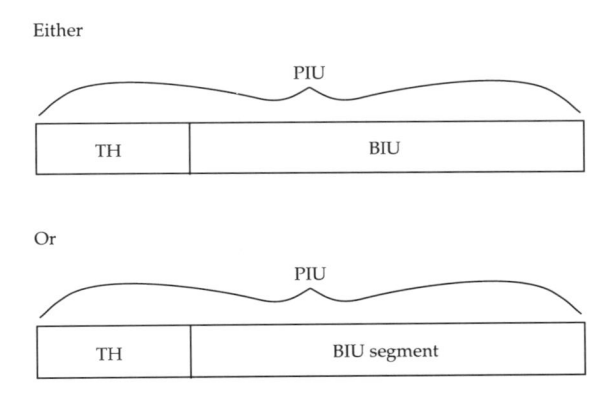

Either

TH	BIU

Or

TH	BIU segment

Figure 31   PIU format

PIU stands for path information unit. A PIU is a **TH** followed by a **BIU** or BIU segment (Fig. 31). See also the section on **units of data**.

Primary LU

The primary **logical unit** or PLU is the LU that sends the **BIND command**. In all terminal-based systems the BIND will come from an application running on the host, so the PLU will always be located in the host. The primary LU is in no way superior to the **secondary LU**; the terminology is only used to identify each end.

Printing

There are two basic types of printing. Screen dumping, where the image on the screen is sent to a printer attached to the same control unit as the screen, and host-addressable printing, where the print is sent from the host. Screen dumping is a function of the control unit, so is not particularly interesting from a communications point of view. This section concentrates on host-addressable printing.

Host-addressable printing is performed using an **LU-LU session**. The **primary LU** is the application that is sending the print, and the **secondary LU** is the printer. The **session type** is usually type 1. The application will normally acquire the printer when it has a print to send and then release it when the print is finished, although this is not always the case.

Typically, there will be no **USS message** 10 sent to the printer, as this is awkward for the printer operators, who would have to re-set the printer to top-of-form. As the application acquires the printer, the first thing that would be seen on a datascope trace is a **BIND command** from the application. An example sequence is in Appendix B.

The difficult part of printing is making sure that the print goes to the correct printer. Applications acquire a particular LU name, which equates to a particular **network address**. Therefore, there is a configuration management issue of ensuring that printer moves correspond with network reconfigurations.

Problems

The purpose of this section is to give a few hints to those who are new to problem solving in a communications environment.

Problems are part of the way of life for communications professionals. They will always occur. The key to problem solving is information. If you know how the system is configured, when it was working, when it stopped working and exactly what the problem is, then you are significantly closer to solving the problem.

Performance problems are addressed in a separate section, so we only consider problems where the system does not do what it should here. There are two basic types of problem: hard, where the system malfunctions consistently in a manner that can be reproduced; and transient, where the problem cannot be reproduced. The two types require different approaches.

Hard problems

The method of debugging hard problems is comparatively straightforward. The key is to find out when the system stopped working and what has been changed between when the system was working and now. This usually gives us a clue as to where the problem lies. When asked what has changed, most users answer 'nothing'. When pushed, they will then start listing the changes that

Protocol conversion 57

have been made but 'would not have affected the problem'. The user is normally a very bad judge of what is relevant. The normal technique is to start by altering the system back to its known working configuration, until the problem goes. It is then normally possible to work out and test the cause of the problem.

Transient problems

The less frequently a transient problem occurs, the more difficult it is to solve. There are two approaches to this type of problem. The first is to continuously monitor the suspected component, and hope that when the error occurs, some useful information on the problem has been recorded. The alternative is to check when the problem has occurred, and then examine any information available, such as system logs, and look for possible clues. It is difficult to say for certain that a transient problem has been fixed. The best way is to keep a record of the occurrences, and assume that a statistically significant reduction in the rate of occurrences is a consequence of action that has been taken to solve the problem.

Some hints

Never believe what you are told. Always check it out for yourself. Good PR is part of the problem diagnosis task. Make sure that the person with the problem knows that you are doing something about it. When the problem is solved, tell everyone.

Protocol conversion

Protocol conversion is the process of 'translating' from a SNA to a non-SNA datastream, typically asynchronous to **SDLC 3270** or **5250**. The device that performs this function is called a protocol converter.

The purpose of the protocol converter is to provide access to an IBM system for a non-IBM device. The advantage of using a protocol converter as opposed to connecting the non-IBM device directly is that the IBM system 'sees' a standard device attached. This simplifies the configuration and operation of the IBM system.

The main reasons for using a protocol converter is price or performance. Protocol converter manufacturers strive to give the user additional functionality at a lower cost.

See Fig. 32 for an example of the use of protocol conversion.

The most common problems that occur with protocol converters concern compatibility with the particular IBM system to which they are connected. The protocol converter will typically provide the PU2 or PU1 functionality in a 3270 or 5250 environment respectively.

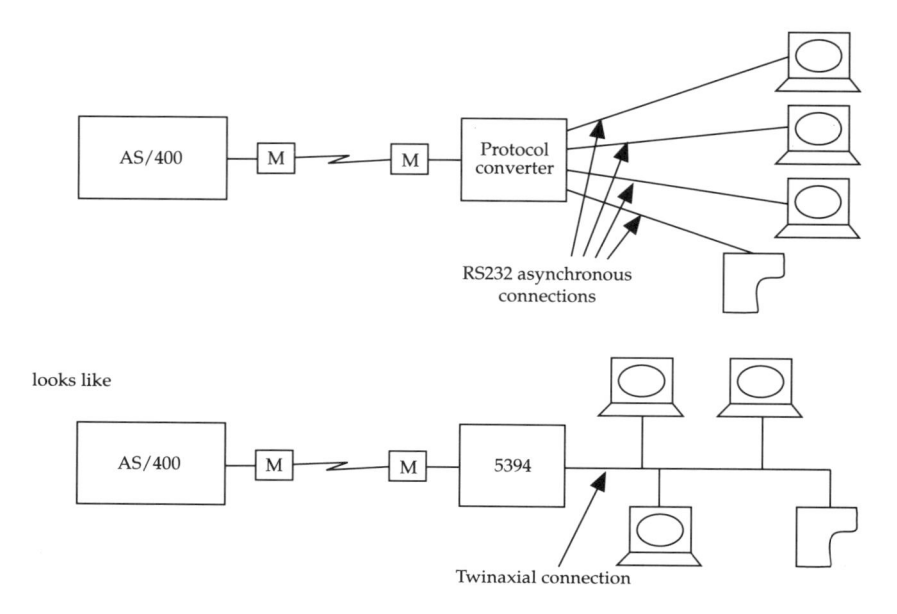

Figure 32 Protocol conversion example

Different manufacturers implement different subsets of the PU functionality, so each PU implementation will behave differently in certain areas. This is also true of IBM—the 3174 does not implement the full PU2 specification as defined in the **FAP manual**. The practical implication of this is that for simple applications, protocol converters will perform the functions required, but in more complicated situations they may not be suitable. They do not perform incorrectly in this case, they just perform differently. The only way of ensuring compatibility with your system is to install a unit and test its functionality. If differences are found between a standard IBM unit, this does not necessarily mean that the protocol converter is wrong. It may be that a change in the host will make the system work properly.

PU2.1

PU2.1 should more properly be referred to as type 2.1 node or T2.1. We will use the terminology T2.1 here.

The most important functionality of T2.1 is as follows:

1. It can connect to other T2.1s, PU4 or PU5.
2. All LU types are supported. Most current implementations only use **LU6.2**, but this is not an architectural limitation.

QLLC 59

However, as T2.1 has been designed to work very closely with LU6.2, in practice LU6.2 will be the most common LU type seen with T2.1.

3. The T2.1 node is managed by a component called the **control point** (CP). When T2.1s are networked, the CPs communicate over an LU6.2 session.
4. T2.1 is the only PU type defined for **SAA**.

T2.1 supports **peer-to-peer** communications, but only when connected to other T2.1s. If the T2.1 is connected to a **boundary function**, then the system becomes hierarchical.

There are three different types of T2.1:

- **LEN end node**
- **APPN end node**
- **APPN network node**

QLLC

QLLC stands for qualified logical link control. It gives direct **X25** support for SNA devices. This includes PU1s, PU2s, **PU2.1s** and PU4s.

The principle of QLLC is simple (Fig. 33). If **SDLC** is being used to transmit a piece of data, the data is enclosed in a 3 byte SDLC **link header** and 3 byte SDLC **link trailer**, and SDLC protocol is used to move the data from one **link station** to the other. In QLLC, the 3 byte SDLC header and trailer are replaced by X25 headers and trailers, and

Compare the SDLC and QLLC datastreams for a PU2.

SDLC

SDLC link header 3 bytes	Transmission header 6 bytes	Request header 3 bytes	Request unit n bytes	SDLC link trailer 3 bytes

QLLC

QLLC header 6 bytes	Transmission header 6 bytes	Request header 3 bytes	Request unit n bytes	QLLC trailer 3 bytes

Figure 33   Basic principle of QLLC

HDLC protocol is used to move the data from one link station to the other. The important point to remember is that the data part is totally independent of the transmission protocol. If we are examining an SDLC trace, we would count 3 bytes in to find the beginning of the **transmission header**. If we are examining a QLLC trace, we would count 6 bytes in to find the beginning of the same transmission header.

With QLLC, most SDLC commands are not transmitted across the link as they are not required. However, certain SDLC commands, for example **XID**, need to be transmitted unchanged. In this case instead of replacing the SDLC header with X25, only the SDLC flag is replaced. The Q bit is set in the packet header, which indicates to the remote link station that the data part of the packet starts with what would have been the **SDLC control field** in an SDLC system. See Fig. 34 for an example of the use of a qualified packet.

It is common for a **PIU** to be significantly larger than the network packet size. In this case, the single PIU is transmitted in multiple X25 packets. This can give rise to a tuning issue in the case of packet networks with a fixed packet size, as it is possible for a significant number of packets to contain a very small number of bytes.

Analysing a QLLC trace is quite straightforward from an SNA perspective. Only examine the I-field. It should start with a transmission header, X'2x' in a PU2 system for example. If this is not the case, the first byte is either an SDLC command transmitted in a qualified packet, or a further part of a **request unit**. It soon becomes obvious from the context.

Compare using SDLC and QLLC to send a set normal response mode (SNRM) command.

SDLC

Byte 0	Byte 1	Byte 2	Bytes 3 and 4	Byte 5
SDLC flag	Station address	SNRM command X '93'	Frame check sequence	SDLC flag

QLLC

Bytes 0-5	Byte 6	Byte 7	Bytes 8 and 9	Byte 10
QLLC header with Q bit set to indicate packet contains control data	Station address	SNRM command X '93'	Frame check sequence	Flag

Figure 34 Use of qualified packets

Requests

Requests are the basic message units sent from one **NAU** to another. There are two basic types of requests:

- requests with SNA commands
- requests with data from **end users**

The format of the request is given in Fig. 35.
See also the sections on **request units** and **request headers**.

Request header	Request unit

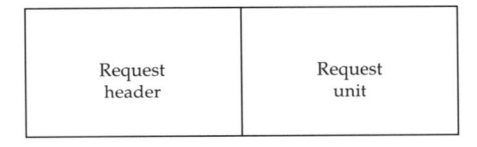

Figure 35   Request format

Request headers

The request header is 3 bytes of control information that precedes a **request unit**. This control information is used by the **NAUs**. The format of the request header is in the IBM formats manual.

Request modes—immediate and delayed

The request mode indicates when an LU can send an **RU** on an **LU-LU session**.

If immediate request mode is used, the sender must wait for a **response** to a particular RU or chain of RUs, before sending the next RU or chain. Immediate request mode can only be used for RUs and chains that require a definite response.

If delayed request mode is used, the sender can send further RUs or RU chains without waiting for a response.

Request units

The request unit is the part of the **request** that contains either data from an **end user** or an SNA command.

62   *Responses*

Example of a data request unit

Consider a **3270** terminal user typing the characters FIND SYSTEM and pressing the enter key. The resultant request unit would contain 3270 information on where the character F was written, an attention identifier indicating that the enter key was pressed, and then the characters FIND SYSTEM.

Example of a command request unit

The **BIND command** activates an **LU-LU session**. When a BIND is sent, the request unit starts with X'31' which indicates that the request unit is a BIND command, and then continues with the BIND command parameters.

Request unit is normally abbreviated to RU. This abbreviation also stands for **response unit**. A bit in the **request header** indicates whether the following RU is a request unit or a response unit.

Responses

Response header	Response unit

Figure 36   Response format

Responses are the basic message units sent between two **NAUs** that acknowledge receipt of **requests**. The format of the response is given in Fig. 36.

Responses can be either positive, indicating that the corresponding request was received and processed correctly, or negative, indicating that the corresponding request was received but not processed correctly.

See also the sections on **response units** and **response headers**.

Response headers

The response header is 3 bytes of control information that precede a **response unit**. This control information is used by the **NAUs**. The format of the response header is in the IBM formats manual.

The response header can also be sent between NAUs without an associated response unit. This mechanism is used to carry **pacing** information, and the type of **response** when definite **response mode** is being used.

Response modes—definite, exception and none

When data is being sent between two LUs, sometimes one will need to know whether the data sent has been received correctly or not.

The response mode, or response protocol as it is more correctly called, relates to how and whether an LU acknowledges receipt of an **RU** from another LU. The **request header** contains the indication of how the RU is to be acknowledged. The acknowledgement is contained in a **response** containing only a **response header**. There are three response modes:

1. In *definite response mode*, every RU will be acknowledged with either a positive or negative response.
2. In *exception response mode*, if the RU has been received and processed correctly, then no acknowledgement is sent. If the RU has been received but not processed correctly, then a negative response will be sent.
3. In *no response mode*, no response will be sent whether the RU was received and processed correctly or not.

The response mode to be used is set in the **BIND command**. No response mode is very rarely used, due to the obvious problems with data integrity. So the choice usually lies between definite and exception response modes. The choice is often restricted by the application used as certain systems must use particular response modes.

It is possible for different response modes to be used during the same **session**.

If definite response mode is used, there are various implications for the network compared to using exception response mode:

1. The number of **BIUs** transmitted is approximately double, as each data BIU will be acknowledged.
2. The distribution of BIU sizes will be significantly altered by the large number of small BIUs transmitted.
3. If immediate **request mode** is used with definite response mode, then throughput will be limited by propagation delays over the network.

Response modes—immediate and delayed

Immediate or delayed response mode indicates whether a LU must send **responses** in the same order in which the corresponding **requests** were received.

If immediate response mode is used, the LU must send responses in the same order in which the requests were received.

If delayed response mode is used, the LU can send responses as soon as the corresponding **RU** has been processed without regard to the order in which they were received.

In most systems in common use today, RUs are processed sequentially by the LU, so the response mode to be used is not particularly relevant. However, in the case of **LU6.2** systems where multiple tasks could be carried out over a single **session**, the response mode used will be relevant to and affect the behaviour of the system.

Response times

Response time is the time taken from when an interactive user hits the enter key to when one of the following three things happen:

1. The first character appears on the screen. This would be applicable, for example, in a system where telephonists are servicing customer enquiries. If we assume that the time taken for the first character to appear on the screen is the same as the time taken for the whole of the first block of data to appear on the screen, then the telephonist can start talking to the customer (for example, confirming the address) with a response time determined by the first character appearing. We assume here that the time for the whole screen to appear is short enough for the telephonist to be able to continue talking. If not, the second response time definition should be used.
2. The last character appears on the screen. This would be applicable in a system where the user requires the whole screen of data before being able to proceed; for example, in a credit control system where the total outstanding is in the bottom right of the screen.
3. The keyboard is unlocked. This would be applicable in a system where the user is entering data and can only proceed when the keyboard is unlocked.

Response times should always be considered in conjunction with the requirements of the user, which will indicate the way response times should be measured, and also the acceptable mean and distribution. Most users require a consistent response time as well as an acceptable mean.

Response units

		Corresponding request	
		SNA command	End user data
Response type	Positive	SNA command code—length 1 or 3 bytes or extended response length up to 30 bytes depending on response	No response unit included in the response
	Negative	Sense code indicating the problem, then the SNA command code	2 or 4 byte sense code

Figure 37 Response unit contents

The response unit is an optional field in the **response**. The format and contents of a response unit are dictated by the corresponding **request unit**. This is summarized in Fig. 37.

Response unit is normally abbreviated to **RU**. This abbreviation also stands for request unit. A bit in the **RH** indicates whether the following RU is a request unit or a response unit.

RH

RH stands for **request header** or **response header**. It is usually obvious from the context whether the R stands for request or response. See also the section on **units of data**.

RTM

RTM stands for response time monitor. It is an IBM software product for measuring, analysing and reporting on the **response times** of certain interactive systems, typically **3270**.

RTM comes in two parts. Software in the **cluster controller** measures and stores response time data for transmission to the host when required. Host software analyses the data and produces reports and alert information for the interactive operator. The host software is either called RTM or **netview performance monitor** depending on how up to date the system is.

The host application communicates with the controller over the **SSCP**-PU session. The NMVT (network management vector transport) command is used.

RU

RU stands for **request unit** or **response unit**. It is usually obvious from the context whether the R stands for request or response. See also the section on **units of data**.

SAA

SAA stands for systems application architecture.

Currently, IBM supplies multiple hardware platforms, each of which runs different operating systems. This presents users with the following:

1. *Multiple database environments*: it is not possible to run a **mainframe** database system on a PS/2.
2. *Multiple application development systems*: a spreadsheet program designed for a PS/2 will not run on an **AS/400**.
3. *Connectivity problems*: it is difficult to make a PS/2 communicate with a **CICS** mainframe application designed for **3270** terminals.
4. *Multiple user interfaces*: the screen presentation on a PS/2 looks entirely different from that of an AS/400. For less literate users, retraining will be required.

Thus users still have the problems of application portability, multiple skill requirements and different user interfaces, even though the equipment comes from one supplier.

SDLC

SAA has been conceived to overcome these problems. The philosophy is similar to that of SNA, but relates to the entire DP system, not just communications. So SAA is a set of rules that all DP systems must conform to. If a particular product conforms to the SAA rules, then in theory it will work on any SAA compatible hardware platform.

SAA defines three standard interfaces as follows:

1. *Common user access*: this defines the rules for the interface between the user and the SAA system, for example keyboard layout.
2. *Common programming interface*: this defines the programming languages that may be used together with database access and management systems.
3. *Common communications support (CCS)*: this defines the communications services that are available for applications to interface with and connect across the network. CCS includes a subset of the SNA architecture, and also some OSI protocols.

SDLC

SDLC stands for synchronous data link control and is the link protocol almost universally used in SNA networks. SDLC provides the data link control **layer** in an SNA system.

SDLC is a master/slave protocol. The master station (primary) polls one or more slave stations (secondary). The secondary stations will only transmit if they have been polled.

SDLC transmissions come in 'lumps' called basic link units (**BLUs**), or **frames**.

Link header 3 bytes			Data to be carried across a link using the SDLC protocol not always present	Link trailer 3 bytes	
Start flag	Station address	Control field		Frame check sequence	End flag

Figure 38   Format of an SDLC BLU

The format of a BLU is given in Fig. 38. The **link header** contains the following:

BYTE 0

Start flag: this marks the start of the BLU. The flag is a unique sequence in the bit stream that is managed by a technique known as zero insertion.

BYTE 1

Station address: this is sometimes called the cluster address or poll address. Please see the section **station address** for more details.

BYTE 3

Control field: this field contains SDLC commands and **responses** which are used to initialize and control the link and to recover from errors. Please see the section **SDLC control field** for more details.

The **link trailer** contains the following:

BYTE 0 and 1

Frame check sequence: the sending **link station** applies a mathematical process to the BLU that generates the FCS. The process is applied in reverse by the receiving link station to check whether the BLU has been received without errors. The probability that this system fails is negligible.

BYTE 3

End flag: this marks the end of the BLU. The format is the same as the start flag. If an SDLC link station is transmitting more than one BLU consecutively, then the end flag will also serve as the start flag for the next BLU. A secondary station will usually be in either normal disconnected mode (not able to send data) or normal **response mode** (able to send data).

SDLC control field

The control field defines the function of the **SDLC BLU**, and will be in one of three formats. The format type is given in the first one or two bits of the control field. The formats and commands are as given below:

Unnumbered format

Unnumbered **frames** are used for establishing and terminating connections between primary and secondary stations on the data **link** and reporting certain errors. This format is also used for transferring data when sequence numbers are not used. The more common commands and **responses** are:

SDLC control field

1. DISC (disconnect): this command is sent from primary to secondary, and places the link in normal disconnected mode.
2. DM (disconnected mode) is the response when the secondary station is in normal disconnected mode. It indicates that the link is ready to be started or re-started. The response from the primary will depend on what the primary wants to do.
3. FRMR (frame reject): This command is sent in response to an invalid frame. The link must then be re-started using SNRM, DISC or SIM. Note that an invalid frame check sequence does not count as an invalid frame.
4. RD (request disconnect): this command is sent by the secondary. It requests that the primary sends a DISC command.
5. SNRM (set normal response mode): this command puts the secondary station into normal **response mode**. The response is UA. Supervisory and information frames can now flow on the link.
6. UA (unnumbered acknowledgement): this is an affirmative response.
7. **XID** (exchange station identification): this command requests information about a secondary station. The response to this is also XID. This response is unique in that data is included in the frame.

Supervisory format

Supervisory frames are used to control the movement of data on the link. The commands can be sent by both the primary and secondary.

1. RR (receive ready): this command confirms the successful receipt of up to seven (or 127 if modulo 128 is used) information frames, and that the station is ready to receive more information frames.
2. RNR (receive not ready): this command confirms the successful receipt of up to seven information frames and that the station is temporarily unable to receive more information frames.
3. REJ (reject): this command is used to request the retransmission of information frames. For example, if a frame is out of sequence then a reject will result.

Information format

Information format frames contain data. They are numbered using number sent (Ns) and number received (Nr) counts. The response will be an information or supervisory frame in which the Nr count equals the number of frames that have been successfully received.

SDLC OR X25?

Using **X25** networks to carry SNA data is a common practice. Most X25 equipment is able to provide either an **SDLC** or an X25 interface to the IBM system, and most IBM systems are able to support SDLC or X25. This section considers some of the issues when making a decision whether to run SDLC or X25 on the IBM. The important point to remember is that it should make no difference to the application. The application is only affected by the LU type, and this is independent of the communications protocol used, as is the PU type.

The reality is that there is seldom any strong reason for either protocol. Operational considerations and the skills of the personnel involved are often deciding factors. For example, if the network operators are familiar with SDLC systems, then that would suggest that an SDLC interface should be used.

The deciding factor is usually cost. Some of the costs to be considered are as follows:

1. *Software costs*: will it be necessary to buy or rent extra software, for example **NPSI**?
2. *CPU cycles*: will one protocol cost us more CPU cycles to run? Will this be a problem? For example using X25 instead of SDLC may increase the CPU utilization on the **FEP** by 30 per cent. This may not be a problem if the current CPU utilization is 20 per cent.
3. *Ports*: how many ports will we require to support the desired number of terminals?
4. *Network bandwidth*: what is the bandwidth requirement of the two options? Will one require more circuits?
5. *Packet throughput*: will one option generate more packets than the other? Will this result in more X25 equipment?
6. *X25 equipment*: X25 equipment is likely to be better at processing X25 as opposed to SDLC. What is the difference in the cost of switches and PADs, etc?

A useful rule of thumb is as follows:

1. If the network is to support a high number of **cluster controllers**, each generating a low volume of data, then X25 is likely to be preferable.
2. If the network is to support a low number of cluster controllers, each generating a high volume of data, then SDLC is likely to be preferable.

Segmenting   71

Secondary LU

The secondary **logical unit** or SLU is the LU that receives the **BIND command**. In all hierarchical systems the BIND will go from the host to the terminal, so the SLU will always be located at the terminal end of the system. The secondary LU is in no way inferior to the **primary LU**—the terminology is only used to identify each end.

Segmenting

We have an RU 800 bytes long to send from a 3745 to a 3174. The maximum BIU size allowed on the SDLC link is 265 bytes (max. data = 265). The BIU is 803 bytes long.

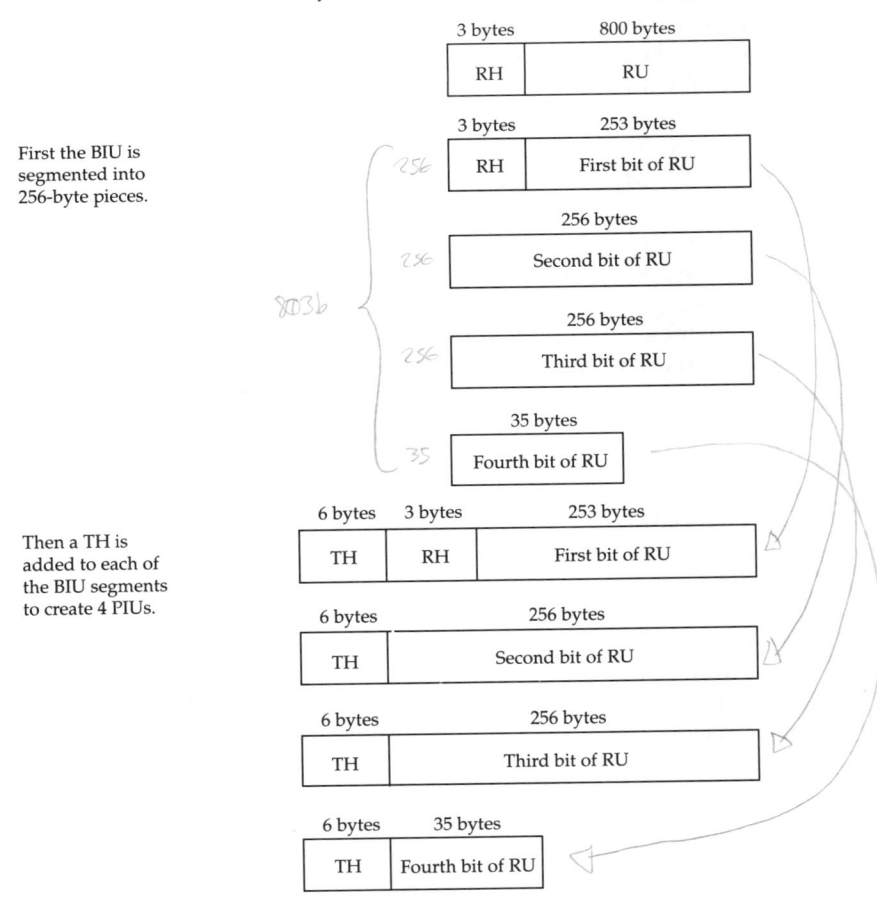

```
                               3 bytes          800 bytes
                              ┌──────┬──────────────────────┐
                              │  RH  │          RU          │
                              └──────┴──────────────────────┘

                               3 bytes          253 bytes
First the BIU is              ┌──────┬──────────────────────┐
segmented into                │  RH  │   First bit of RU    │
256-byte pieces.              └──────┴──────────────────────┘

                                       256 bytes
                                    ┌──────────────────────┐
                                    │   Second bit of RU   │
                                    └──────────────────────┘

                                       256 bytes
                                    ┌──────────────────────┐
                                    │   Third bit of RU    │
                                    └──────────────────────┘

                                       35 bytes
                                    ┌──────────┐
                                    │ Fourth bit of RU │
                                    └──────────┘

                        6 bytes   3 bytes     253 bytes
                       ┌──────┬──────┬──────────────────────┐
Then a TH is           │  TH  │  RH  │   First bit of RU    │
added to each of       └──────┴──────┴──────────────────────┘
the BIU segments
to create 4 PIUs.       6 bytes           256 bytes
                       ┌──────┬──────────────────────┐
                       │  TH  │   Second bit of RU   │
                       └──────┴──────────────────────┘

                        6 bytes           256 bytes
                       ┌──────┬──────────────────────┐
                       │  TH  │   Third bit of RU    │
                       └──────┴──────────────────────┘

                        6 bytes   35 bytes
                       ┌──────┬──────────┐
                       │  TH  │ Fourth bit of RU │
                       └──────┴──────────┘
```

Then the 4 PIUs are transmitted across the link in 4 BLUs.

Figure 39   Segmenting example

Segmenting is the process of chopping up a **BIU** (into segments) before adding the **TH** to it to create **PIUs** (Fig. 39). Segmenting is most commonly performed between a communications controller and a **cluster controller**, as the PIU size is much greater than the maximum **BLU** size allowed on the **link**.

Sense data

If a problem occurs in an SNA system the relevant resources will be informed if possible. Typically this is with a negative response to a request. Wherever possible, 2 or 4 bytes of additional information are included. These characters are called the sense codes or sense data.

The sense code should be looked up in the relevant manual—the **FAP manual** contains a complete list of codes, although certain product specific manuals are more easy to use. The explanation given should specify or point to the problem area.

Sequences

When examining a trace in a problem solving situation, it is necessary to know the sequences of commands that would occur in a working system.

Appendix B gives some of the more common command sequences. Further details can be found in the IBM formats manual.

Sessions

Two **NAUs** are in session when they are 'talking' to each other. A session is defined as the temporary connection over which two NAUs communicate.

Sessions are temporary in that SNA defines a way of activating and deactivating a session. However, a session may last a very long time. There is nothing to stop a session from lasting until a failure of the network occurs. We hope, of course, that this will be a long time.

The types of session defined by SNA are:

- **SSCP**-PU, activated by the ACTPU command
- SSCP-LU, activated by the ACTLU command
- SSCP-SSCP, activated by the ACTCDRM command
- **LU-LU**, activated by the **BIND command**
- CP-CP, activated by the BIND command

Note that PU-LU and PU-PU sessions are not allowed.

CP-CP sessions are only relevant in a network with **PU2.1**.

Session setup is always controlled by the SSCP in a **mainframe** system. For an SSCP-LU or SSCP-PU session to be set up, the SSCP must first be in session with all the resources above the LU or PU in the **hierarchy**.

When **VTAM** is in session with a resource, the VTAM display will give the resource status as ACTIV or ACT/n where n is B,C,S or U.

Session level pacing

Session level pacing is used to control the rate at which data is transmitted on an **LU-LU session**. The reason that this mechanism is required is that an LU may be able to send data much faster than the other LU may be able to process it; for example, **file transfer** from a **mainframe** to a PC.

Session level pacing operates on the **half session**, so for a given LU-LU session, the **pacing** parameters can be different for data transmissions in each direction. This is almost always the case in a properly tuned mainframe system, as the host is invariably fast compared to the terminal devices.

Session level pacing can be done in one or two stages. In two stage pacing, the flow is paced between one LU and a **boundary function** (typically an **NCP**); and also between the boundary function and the other LU. The pacing parameters can be, and often are, different for each stage. In one stage pacing, there is no intermediate stage, the LUs pace directly between each other. The advantage of two stage pacing is that, in a properly tuned system, **response times** and throughput can be optimized.

Session types

Session type is short for **LU-LU session** type. It means the same thing as **logical unit type**. The reason for the two different terms meaning the same thing is that a particular LU can often support different LU-LU session types. The term LU type implies that an LU cannot change the type of **end user** it supports, so this can lead to confusion.

SNA—what exactly is it?

SNA is a structured set of rules governing the management of a communications network. 'Communications network' means everything from the write command in an application program to the screen drivers in the terminal. This must be contrasted with OSI, where the term network relates only to the functions that move data. 'Management' means anything that needs to be done in order to get the data from one end of the network to the other.

The whole point of SNA is that it is a standard. So if two products conform to the SNA standard, then they should work together. Products conform to SNA—not the other way around. Virtually every new communications product that IBM has produced over the past 15 years has been designed to conform to the SNA rules (or **architecture**).

SNA is big. Prior to **SAA**, SNA was reputed to be IBM's biggest investment ever.

The SNA rules are still evolving, **APPN** being a case in point. However, this does not mean that 'old' SNA will not work with 'new' SNA. IBM has a policy of upwards compatibility, which means that (within reason) new products will work with older products. The IBM 3278 terminal is well over 15 years old which is prehistoric in data processing terms. However, it is compatible with the most up to date hardware. That is a fairly simple idea, but it illustrates how successful the principle of SNA is.

SNI

SNI stands for SNA network interconnection. It is the system used to connect SNA networks together.

Joining two separate SNA networks into a single network, for example after two companies merge, can be an extremely complex exercise. The following problems must be overcome:

1. Coordination of unique names for cross-domain resources throughout the network.
2. **Subarea** numbers must be unique throughout the whole network.
3. There are a number of critical sizing and performance parameters that must be unique in the network.

Connecting SNA networks together is becoming more common as the requirements of network users become more sophisticated. The

Spoofing

purpose of SNI is to avoid the problems involved in connecting SNA networks together, and also to simplify the process.

SNA networks are connected using a gateway. A gateway comprises a gateway **VTAM** and a gateway **NCP**. The gateway provides the functions required to start and stop the SNI connection and to allow cross network **LU-LU sessions**.

Spoofing

Spoofing is a method of using an **X25** network to carry SNA data, while allowing the system to use **SDLC**.

The IBM system is generated for an SDLC circuit. The PAD at the host end emulates a secondary **link station**, responding to SDLC commands. When an SDLC **BLU** that contains an I-field is sent to the PAD, the I-field is packetized and transmitted across the network.

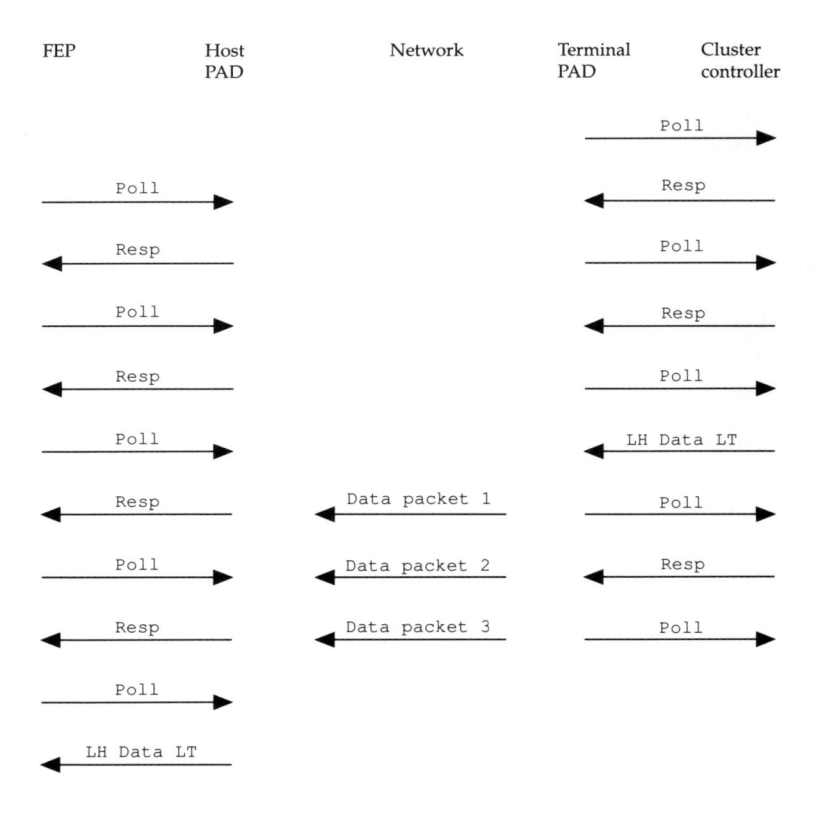

```
FEP         Host         Network         Terminal      Cluster
            PAD                          PAD           controller

                                                   Poll
                                                  ───────►

            Poll                             Resp
           ──────►                          ◄──────

            Resp                             Poll
           ◄──────                          ──────►

            Poll                             Resp
           ──────►                          ◄──────

            Resp                             Poll
           ◄──────                          ──────►

            Poll                          LH Data LT
           ──────►                          ◄──────

            Resp      Data packet 1          Poll
           ◄──────    ◄──────────────       ──────►

            Poll      Data packet 2          Resp
           ──────►    ──────────────►       ◄──────

            Resp      Data packet 3          Poll
           ◄──────    ◄──────────────       ──────►

            Poll
           ──────►

         LH Data LT
         ◄──────────
```

Figure 40   Example of spoofing

The important point to remember is that SDLC receive ready polls and **responses** are not transmitted.

The terminal PAD emulates an SDLC primary station, polling the controller. When it receives an I-field from the network, it depacketizes the I-field, adds the SDLC information to convert it to a BLU and sends it to the controller. This is illustrated in Fig. 40.

The advantage of spoofing is that the IBM system can be generated for SDLC, so is standard from the system point of view. Spoofing is also efficient when the X25 network provider charges by the number of packets transmitted. The non-productive SDLC polls are not transmitted across the network, thus saving on packets transmitted.

The exact way that spoofing works depends on the particular manufacturers implementation. Different manufacturers implement different features, but the basic method of operation remains the same.

Spoofing can also be used to carry any data that would normally be transmitted across an SDLC circuit. This includes PU4-PU4 traffic and **5250 cluster controller** traffic.

Spoofing is most common in X25 networks, but any equivalent system can be used. Ethernet and TCP/IP products also spoof. The principles remain the same.

SSCP

SSCP stands for system services control point. The SSCP is a special kind of PU that has control of part of the network called a **domain**. The number of domains is equal to the number of SSCPs, and all parts of the network must be in a domain.

VTAM is an implementation of SSCP for **mainframe** systems. VTAM 'knows about' and can control all its resources, applications, terminals, etc.

The SSCP is contained in a PU type 5. It is unclear from the SNA rules what parts of the PU5 functionality are not implemented in SSCP, but this distinction is not relevant in the everyday world.

For practical purposes the words SSCP, PU5 and VTAM mean exactly the same, and can be used interchangeably.

Standard systems

In a complicated network, for example one with high-speed multiplexors, **X25** and PC equipment, it is often difficult to determine the

Standard systems

The real hardware is:

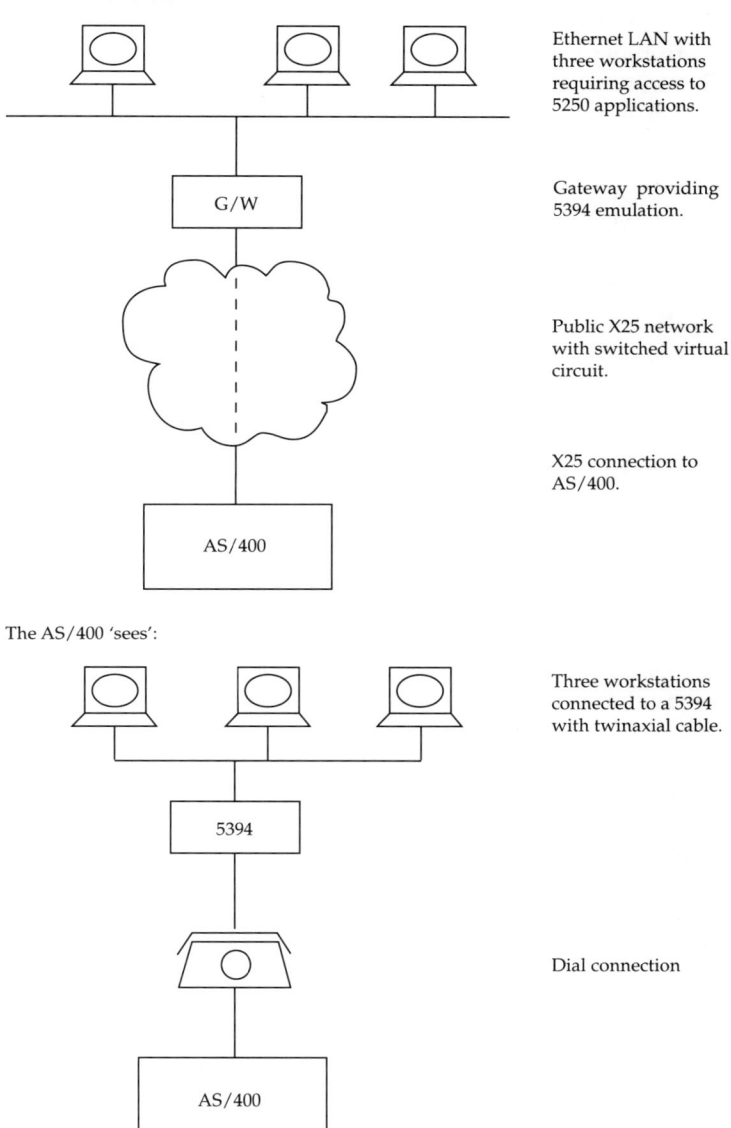

Ethernet LAN with three workstations requiring access to 5250 applications.

Gateway providing 5394 emulation.

Public X25 network with switched virtual circuit.

X25 connection to AS/400.

The AS/400 'sees':

Three workstations connected to a 5394 with twinaxial cable.

Dial connection

Figure 41   Example of standard systems

SNA functionality involved. This can lead to difficulties with problem diagnosis or design work. To get around this, the critical question is often 'what does the IBM think is out there?' Usually, we will have something that performs the functionality of one of a number of standard IBM systems. The more common standard IBM systems are given below:

1. 3767 terminal connected to the **FEP** using a leased circuit.
2. 3767 terminal connected to the FEP using a dial **SDLC** circuit.
3. 3174 **cluster controller** connected to the FEP using a leased SDLC circuit.
4. 3174 cluster controller connected to the FEP using a dial SDLC circuit.
5. 3745 connected to an FEP using a leased SDLC circuit.
6. 3745 connected to the FEP using a dial SDLC circuit.
7. 5394 connected to **AS/400** using a leased SDLC circuit.
8. 5394 connected to AS/400 using a dial SDLC circuit.

'The IBM' in this case normally means **VTAM** or the communications part of the operating system in an AS/400 environment (Fig. 41). The point is that VTAM, AS/400 and the applications neither know nor care about networking protocols or technology. This is one of the strengths of SNA, as the networking technology and protocols have no effect on the access method. VTAM, AS/400 or the applications 'see' one of the standard systems listed above.

Starting a printer session

As printers rarely have a keyboard, it is normal for an **LU-LU session** to be started by an application acquiring the printer. An example sequence is given in Appendix B.

Most applications will only go into session with a printer when they have data to send. Once the print has been completed the session is usually deactivated.

Starting a terminal session

There are three basic methods of starting an **LU-LU session** where one of the LUs is an interactive terminal with a keyboard:

1. The terminal user sends a **request** to the **SSCP** indicating that an LU-LU session is required with a particular application.
2. An application acquires the terminal LU.

3. A **network solicitor** is used, and this application initiates the setting up of an LU-LU session.

An example **sequence** is given in Appendix B.

Station address

This is located in byte number 1 of the **SDLC link header**. It refers to the address of the secondary station on the link, a group address or a broadcast address. The secondary station will only respond to an SDLC **frame** if the address in the frame sent by the primary matches its configured address. Exceptions exist, of course, and are as follows:

1. The address used is the broadcast address (X'FF). All secondary stations will respond to this whatever their configured address.
2. The address used is a group address of a group to which the secondary station belongs. Group addressing is rarely used.
3. Echo defeat is being used. This is an IBM fix to 37xx **FEP** code which forces the primary and secondary stations to use different station addresses. If this is the case, then the most significant bit will be different on the receive and transmit directions. All other bits will be the same. For example, the **NCP** may use station address X'01' and the PU will reply with a station address of X'81'.

Usually, the station addresses will be the same in both transmit and receive directions. The normal standards are to use either X'01' or X'C1'.

Subareas

Subareas are a way of logically dividing a network into smaller parts. A subarea is:

- either a PU4 together with its attached **peripheral nodes**
- or a PU5 together with its attached peripheral nodes

Subareas do not overlap. In practice, every **VTAM** and every **NCP** is a subarea.

Each subarea is assigned a subarea number that must be unique within the whole network. The subarea number is used as part of the **network address** (Fig. 42) on page 80.

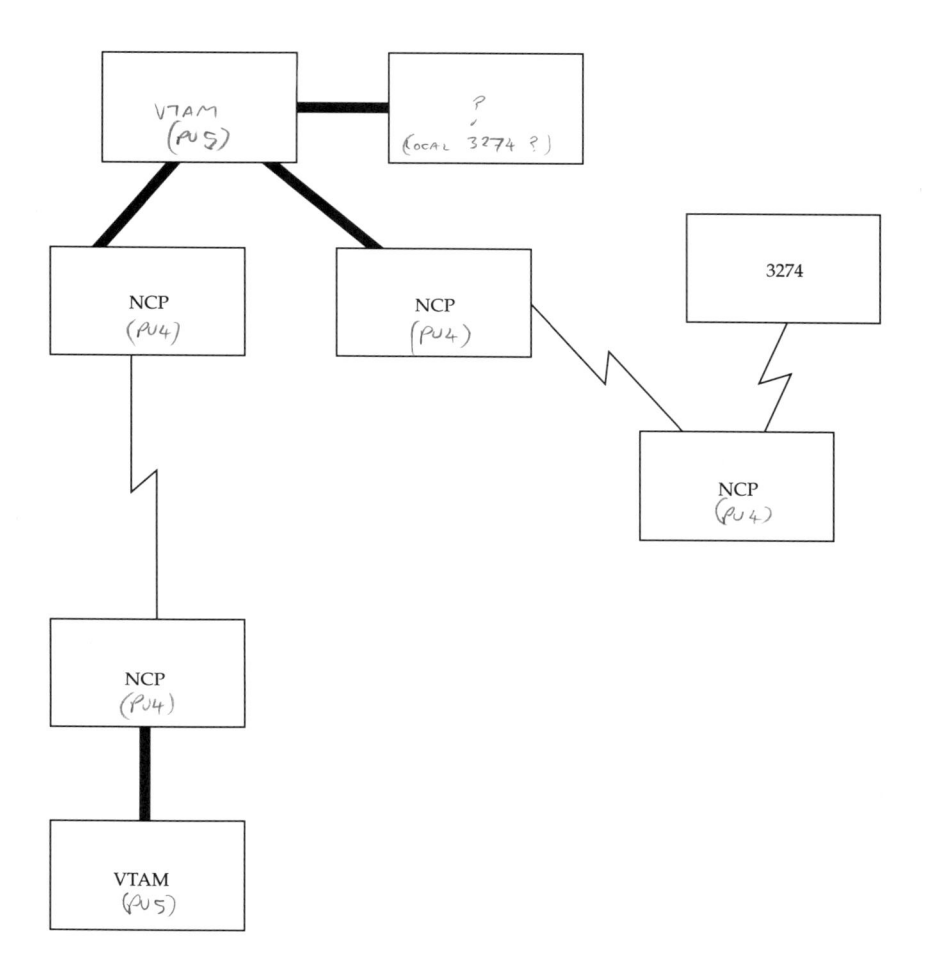

[Figure: network diagram showing VTAM (PU5) connected to a local 3274(?) and to two NCPs (PU4); one NCP (PU4) connects down through another NCP (PU4) to a VTAM (PU5); another NCP (PU4) connects via link to an NCP (PU4) attached to a 3274.]

This network has six subareas — two PU5s and four PU4s.

Figure 42   Subareas

Subarea node

A subarea node is either a **host node**, or a **communication controller node**, i.e. a subarea node will contain either a PU4 or a PU5.

The phrase 'subarea node' is used to distinguish between subarea and **peripheral nodes**. Subarea nodes are distinguished by the fact that they use the **network address** to make routing decisions.

System request key

The system request key is a special key on **3270** terminal keyboards. When a terminal is in **LU-LU session**, then any keyboard input is normally sent on the LU-LU session, i.e. to the application.

The system request key is used to send data on the **SSCP**-LU session. It acts as a toggle switch. Pressing it once 'connects' the terminal to the SSCP-LU session, so terminal input goes to the SSCP. Pressing it again 'connects' the terminal to the LU-LU session, so terminal input goes to the application LU.

Use of the system request key does not de-activate the LU-LU session. It still exists, although the terminal LU usually informs the application LU that it is temporarily unable to accept data.

The system request key is not normally used by ordinary terminal users, although it can be useful for problem diagnosis in some circumstances. If the terminal is getting no **response** from an application, and it is not obvious whether there is a communications or application problem, then the system request key can be used. If it is possible to transmit and receive from the SSCP, then communications are working and the problem probably lies with the application.

It can be difficult to disconnect from applications, especially if you are in a mess, forgetting a password for example. If the system request key is used to 'connect' the terminal to the SSCP-LU session, then the command 'logoff' can be used to de-activate the LU-LU session. In this case, the application has no choice but to drop the **session**.

S/3X

The S/34, S/36 and S/38 are the older IBM products that have now been replaced by the **AS/400** range. From a communications point of view, they are similar to the AS/400. Please see the section on the **AS/400**.

TH

TH stands for **transmission header**. See also the section on **units of data**.

Token ring

Token ring is IBM's strategic LAN offering. It provides the data **link** control **layer** in an SNA system; so from an SNA point of view, token ring is simply a method for moving data around, functionally equivalent to **SDLC** for example.

Most IBM communications devices now have the option of a token ring interface.

Traffic volumes

Accurate traffic volumes are essential if an efficient network is to be designed and run. The problem is that while network designers require peak data bytes per second, the user will give utilization using a totally different unit of measure over a much longer period. For example, users may quote their measure of work rate as television sets sold per day.

In order to calculate the traffic volume figures that can be used for network design, firstly the user's unit of work must be evaluated to determine how much data is transmitted and then the peak rate of transmission must be estimated. The problem is that the peak is usually significantly greater than the average. A useful rule of thumb in a typical system is that during the peak hour a total of 20 per cent of the daily traffic will be generated. This is almost double the mean rate.

There is no special formula for calculating traffic volumes for a network design. The basic steps are as follows:

1. Understand the user's business.
2. Calculate the peak workload in the same units that the user uses.
3. Translate from the user's units of work to data bits transmitted.

It is rarely useful to calculate to many decimal places, as the ultimate answer required is usually 'How many circuits do we require to support this user population?'

Transaction

Different people define a transaction in different ways:

1. *Definition 1*. A transaction is a single interactive message pair.
2. *Definition 2*. A transaction is a **logical unit** of work. For example, this could be recording a customer's payment at a public utility company. The sequence of events would be: first, pulling up the payment screen; then, entering the customer's name, which would then result in the customer's details being displayed; and then, entering the payment details. This definition of a transaction results in three message pairs for this particular transaction.

Applications programmers also talk about transactions. In this context, transaction means a routine or program that is called to perform a particular task; this is effectively definition 2.

Transaction program

There are two areas in which the phrase 'transaction program' is used. The first is in interactive systems, where transaction program is used to refer to the code that processes **transactions**. The second and more important use, which is discussed in this section, relates to **APPC**.

A transaction program is a piece of code that uses SNA to communicate with other transaction programs. The SNA rules used are almost invariably **LU6.2**. The important thing about transaction programs is that they are written by application programmers to do useful work. Transaction programs are the **end users** in an LU6.2 environment.

See also the section on **conversations**.

Transmission group

A transmission group is a group of **links** between adjacent **subareas** that appear as a single logical connection to path control (Fig. 43). This means that from a routeing point of view, we route data across a transmission group and do not care how many links there are in the transmission group. Data to be sent across a particular transmission

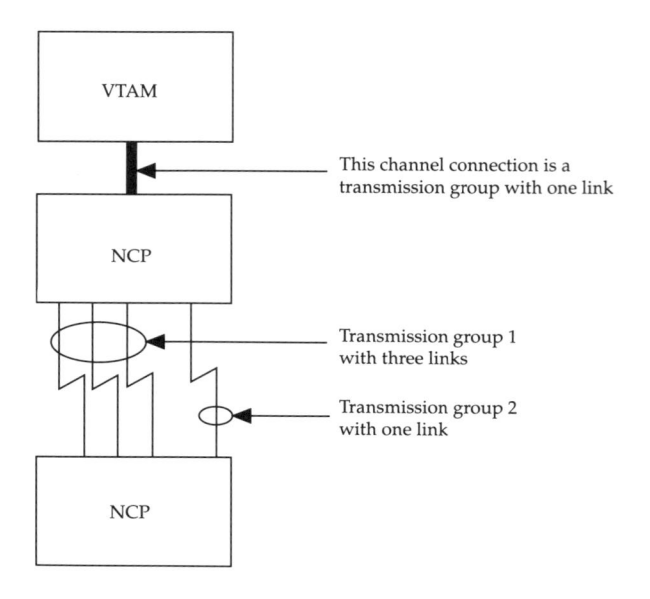

Figure 43 Transmission group example

group is queued and then sent across the first link in the transmission group that becomes free. The data is then dequeued and re-sequenced, and sent on its way in the original sequence.

There are two advantages with multiple link transmission groups. Firstly, multiple links give extra bandwidth. Secondly, a multiple link transmission group is more resilient. In the event of a link failure in a multiple link transmission group, the transmission group remains intact and no **sessions** or data are lost. Sessions only fail when the final link in a multiple link transmission group fails.

Note that in a multiple link transmission group, it is strongly recommended that link speeds and propagation delays are all identical. Adding slower links will certainly lead to inefficiencies and may in some circumstances result in increased **response times**. It would be better to add the slower links on an additional transmission group and route some session traffic over that transmission group to reduce the load on the faster transmission group.

Transmission header

The transmission header is a string of control bytes created and used by the path control **layer** to route information from its origin **NAU** to its destination NAU. The format of the **TH** varies according to its use and is identified in the first half of the first byte of the TH.

The format ID or FID identifies the format and use of transmission headers. The most common are as follows:

1. FID 2: used to route data between a **subarea node** and an adjacent PU type 2 or **PU type 2.1**; or between two PU type 2.1s.
2. FID3: used to route data between a subarea node and an adjacent PU type 1.
3. FID4: used to route data between adjacent subarea nodes when both support **explicit route** protocols and **virtual route** protocols.

Transmission priority

A transmission priority (TP) is assigned to data flowing over an **explicit route**. There are three priorities; 0 is the lowest, 1 is the middle and 2 is the highest. Data with a high TP is transmitted before data with a lower TP. **Subarea nodes** have an ageing algorithm which ensures that data with the lowest TP is not held up indefinitely. The **class of service** table points to the TP that is to be used by a particular **LU-LU session**.

There is also a network priority that is used to send SNA commands and **pacing** information. This is higher than TP2, and is only used by the network.

TSO

TSO stands for time sharing option. It is an interactive system that gives users access to the MVS operating system and can be used for operating system tasks, for example, allocating space on disks or submitting batch jobs. Most TSO systems will also have ISPF which is a full screen editor with features such as text editing, simplified DASD management and access to **JES** and MVS facilities. All MVS environments will run TSO and most will also have ISPF.

From an SNA point of view, TSO is a **VTAM** application. There is a **logical unit** for the main TSO task and one logical unit per additional simultaneous user. Each of these must be defined in the TSO **major node**. When an **LU-LU session** with TSO is activated, the initial **BIND command** comes from the main TSO task. After a positive response from the terminal LU, an UNBIND is immediately issued and then a BIND is issued by the first available TSO user task. If this is successful a start data traffic command follows and then the first data message from TSO, probably 'enter user ID'. This sequence of BIND, UNBIND, BIND can cause problems in some single terminal situations with OEM equipment where the system assumes that the first UNBIND means that the connection is no longer required and consequently terminates the connection. TSO will support both **session type** 1 and session type 2. Session type 1 is used for both interactive and **printing** applications. Session type 2 (**3270**) is, of course, interactive only.

Tuning

Tuning is the process of improving a network's performance without spending money on hardware or additional software. It is a large and complicated subject. The process of tuning consists of altering network parameters and then deciding whether the performance of the network is 'better' or 'worse' than before. The important points to remember when tuning a network are as follows:

1. Only change one thing at a time.
2. Make sure that you are thoroughly familiar with the 'before' situation. This will normally involve taking measurements over a long period of time.
3. Have a clear goal in mind. Tuning is invariably a trade-off. In a heavily used network the improvement in service that some users receive, may result in a degradation of service to other users. For example, improving interactive **response time** may result in increasing the time taken to print reports. This may or may not be 'better'. It all depends on the requirements of the users.

Units of data

As data traverses an SNA network, its format and the control information added to the data change. Each of these particular formats has a specific name. Figure 44 illustrates these different formats.

The following acronyms are used:

- RU   Request/response unit
- RH   Request/response header
- BIU   Basic information unit

Units of data

Application performs a write command	[RU]
The RH is added by transmission control	BIU = [RH	RU]

either / or

- The BIU is cut into segments: [BIU segment]
- and then a TH is added to each BIU segment: PIU = [TH | BIU segment]
- or a TH is added to the BIU: PIU = [TH | BIU]

[PIU]

- either the PIU is blocked with other PIUs: BTU = [PIU | PIU]
- or the PIU is not blocked with other PIUs: BTU = [PIU]

[BTU]

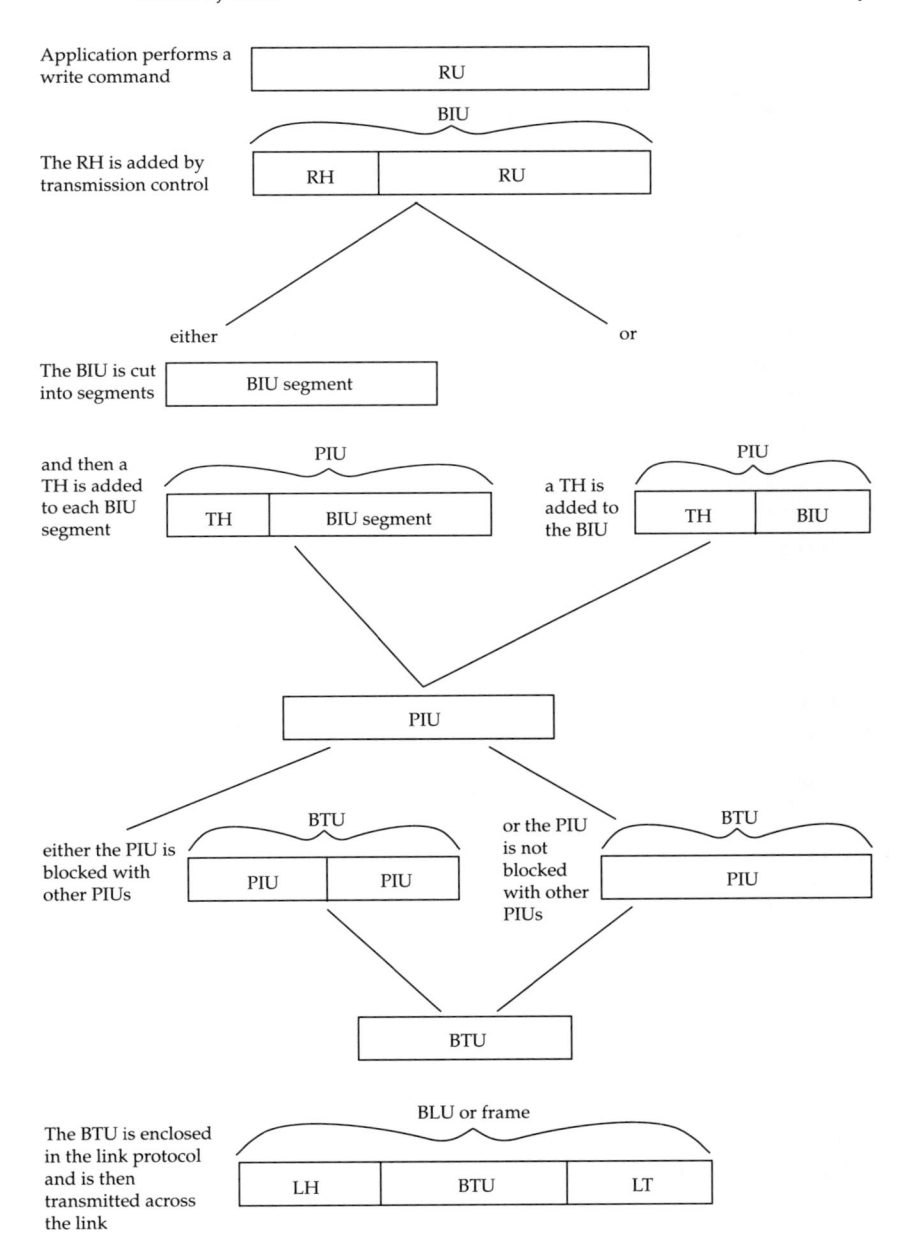

The BTU is enclosed in the link protocol and is then transmitted across the link: BLU or frame = [LH | BTU | LT]

Figure 44   Units of data

- TH   Transmission header
- PIU Path information unit
- BTU Basic telecommunications unit
- BLU Basic link unit

USS

USS stands for unformatted system services. It refers to the **VTAM** functionality that provides a basic user interface, providing commands for starting and stopping terminal to application sessions, and giving the terminal user basic information.

USS commands

USS commands refer to the commands that a terminal user may send to **VTAM** to ask VTAM to do something. USS commands are sent on the **SSCP**-LU session. There are three commands as given below:

LOGON

This command requests VTAM to start an **LU-LU session** with the requested LU. The format of the command is as follows:

    LOGON APPLID(AAA) LOGMODE(LLL) DATA(DDD)

AAA specifies the application LU, LLL the **logmode** and DDD the data that is to be passed to the application.

LOGOFF

This command requests the termination of an LU-LU session. The format of the command is as follows:

    LOGOFF APPLID(AAA) TYPE(COND/UNCOND) HOLD(YES/NO)

AAA specifies the application LU, the TYPE setting determines if the application is forced to terminate the **session** unconditionally, and HOLD determines if the PU is to be disconnected when the last terminal has logged off.

IBMTEST

This command requests that a number of echo messages are sent from VTAM to the terminal. It is useful to determine whether there are any major communication problems or not. The format of the command is as follows:

    IBMTEST NN

NN specifies the number of echo messages that are to be sent to the terminal.

Note that certain systems delimit the logon and logoff parameters with = rather than enclosing them in brackets. All the parameters do not have to be entered; they can be allowed to default.

USS messages

USS messages are written by **VTAM** to terminal devices to give the terminal user basic information about what is going on. The default messages supplied by IBM are not particularly user-friendly, although it is possible to customize these messages to make them more informative. The messages are described in the VTAM messages and codes manual, and customization in the VTAM installation manual.

USS messages are sent on the **SSCP**-LU session, so if a USS message is displayed on a terminal, physical communications must be working.

The most common USS messages are as follows. The default IBM messages are given; 'Installation dependent message' means that there is no message in the default tables.

    Message0 Installation dependent message

This indicates that the command that the terminal user entered was syntactically correct and that VTAM is processing the command.

    Message1 INVALID COMMAND SYNTAX

This means that the syntax of the command entered at the terminal was incorrect.

    Message2 xxxxxx COMMAND UNRECOGNIZED

This means that the command entered at the terminal was incorrect. xxxxxx indicates the command that VTAM did not recognize.

    Message4 Pn PARAMETER INVALID

The command and the syntax were correct. However, the nth parameter of the command was not correct for some reason. The most common form of this message is P1 PARAMETER INVALID. This means that the application requested is not known to VTAM.

Message5 UNSUPPORTED FUNCTION

This means that the terminal LU sent a command to VTAM in an improper manner. Typically this is because a PF or PA key was pressed when in SSCP-LU session. Only Enter, Clear or Sys Request are valid.

Message6 SEQUENCE ERROR

Either a logoff command was sent when there was no **LU-LU session**, or a logon **request** was sent when there was already an LU-LU session in existence.

Message7 SESSION NOT BOUND
or   xxxx UNABLE TO ESTABLISH SESSION, RU_yyyy
            FAILED WITH SENSE zzzz

The format of this message depends on the release of VTAM. Almost invariably this means that a valid logon request was entered for an **active** application, and the application did not allow the **session** setup to proceed. With the second format, xxxx gives the LU name, yyyy the command that failed, and zzzz the sense code.

Message10 Installation dependent message

This indicates that the terminal has successfully been activated.

Message13 IBM ECHO ABCD . . . XYZ 1234567890

This is the **response** to the IBMTEST command.

USS tables

USS tables are used to improve the terminal user interface to **VTAM**. The format of the **USS** logon command is as follows:

LOGON APPLID(AAA) LOGMODE(LLL) DATA(DDD)

This command is requesting a **session** with the application called AAA using a logon mode of LLL and passing the data DDD to the application. This system is cumbersome and difficult for users to understand. In most **mainframe** systems, therefore, a customized USS table is provided to allow a comparatively simple command to be translated into the full logon **request** string. For example, a typical translate customization would translate **TSO** into:

LOGON APPLID(A05TSO) LOGMODE(M32782)

USS tables are also used to translate **USS messages** into something

VTAM

more meaningful. For example USS message 4 P1 PARAMETER INVALID could be translated into 'You have requested an unknown application'. Further information on USS tables is contained in the VTAM installation guide.

Virtual routes

A virtual route is a logical connection between two **subareas**. The two subareas in question do not have to be adjacent. **Session** traffic is routed over a particular virtual route.

Virtual routes are mapped to **explicit routes** that define the physical routeing.

A **transmission priority** is always associated with a virtual route.

Virtual route pacing

Virtual route pacing controls the rate of flow of data between the two end **subareas** on a **virtual route**. See also the section on **pacing**. The routines that set and alter the pacing window size are usually supplied by IBM. These are normally perfectly adequate. However, it is possible to customize these routines in special circumstances, although this is unusual.

VM

VM stands for virtual machine. It is the IBM **mainframe** operating system that allows a single physical mainframe to be split into multiple logical mainframes.

VM can run **VTAM** direct or use an operating system such as MVS or VSE, with VTAM under that (Fig. 45). The important thing from an SNA point of view is how many VTAMs are running in a machine. This gives us the number of **domains**.

VTAM

VTAM stands for virtual telecommunications access method. It is the **mainframe** software that controls part of a network, and provides the interface between the network and the application programs. VTAM provides the **SSCP** functionality from an SNA perspective. VTAM runs under all versions of MVS, and also **VM** and VSE.

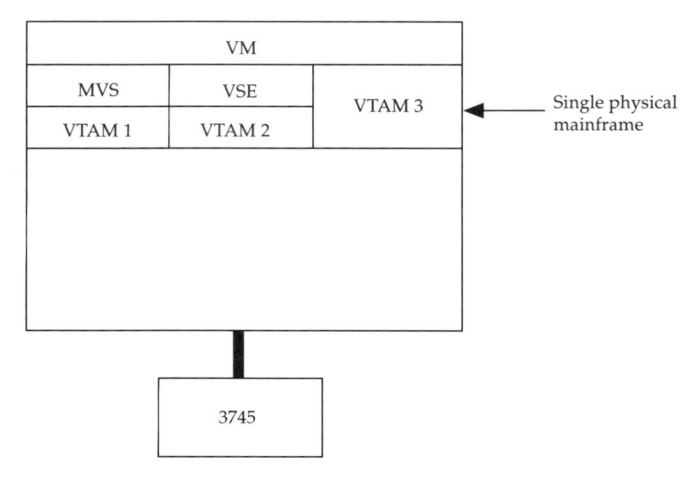

VTAM applications

```
+---------------------------------------+
|                 VM                    |
+--------+--------+                     |
|  MVS   |  VSE   |      VTAM 3         |  ← Single physical
+--------+--------+                     |    mainframe
| VTAM 1 | VTAM 2 |                     |
+--------+--------+---------------------+
|                                       |
|                                       |
|                                       |
+--------------------+------------------+
                     |
                 +-------+
                 | 3745  |
                 +-------+
```

This is the same from an SNA point of view as:

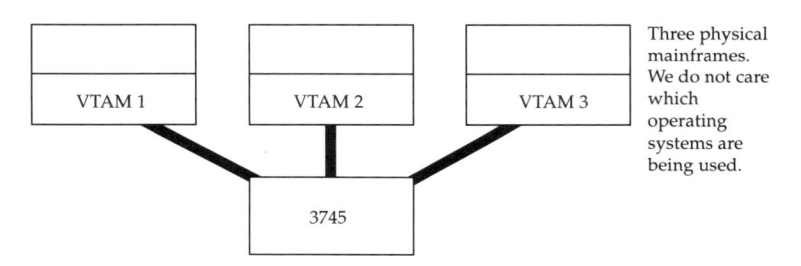

```
+--------+      +--------+      +--------+
| VTAM 1 |      | VTAM 2 |      | VTAM 3 |
+--------+      +--------+      +--------+
     \             |               /
      \            |              /
       \        +-------+        /
        \------ | 3745  | ------/
                +-------+
```

Three physical mainframes. We do not care which operating systems are being used.

Figure 45   VM

As all the traffic generated by the network passes through the VTAM code, tuning of VTAM in a heavily loaded system is critical.

VTAM generates messages to inform the VTAM operator what is going on, and receives and processes **VTAM commands** from the operator. In a typical network, all the VTAM messages will go to the **netview** console, and this will be used to enter VTAM commands.

VTAM applications

VTAM application, or simply, application is the term that SNA systems programmers use to describe the pieces of code that run under the control of VTAM and provide the LU functionality. See Fig. 20 on page 36. **CICS** and **TSO** are examples of VTAM applications, and VTAM will refer to them as APPLS.

Care needs to be taken when talking to other DP people as some would consider CICS, for example, to be a major subsystem, and refer to the user generated code which searches for name and address and presents it on a 3270 screen to be the application.

VTAM commands

VTAM commands are typically entered from either the operating system console or the **netview** console. There are three main types of command as given below.

Vary

Vary commands change the status of resources. The correct terminology is to vary a resource **active**, or vary it inactive. The terminology 'varying online or offline' relates to operating system peripherals; and varying up, on, down or off does not relate to much at all.

Display

Display commands tell you what **VTAM** knows about the resource. The result of a display command is a number of VTAM messages that give all the information on a particular resource, including the **VTAM state**.

Modify

Modify commands control some of the VTAM operating and diagnostic functions. The most common use of the modify command is starting and stopping traces.

All VTAM commands are detailed in the VTAM operation manual.

VTAM datasets

When **VTAM** is running, it uses a number of datasets that are pointed to by the VTAM JCL. The two most interesting contain a description of the network, and various tables coded by the systems programmer that are used by VTAM. The names of the datasets are installation dependent, but they are almost invariably referred to as VTAMLST and VTAMLIB.

VTAMLIB

This contains **logmode** tables, **class of service** tables, and **USS tables**. IBM supply default tables, although most installations add their own.

VTAMLST

This contains a description of the network. Each **major node** is a member of the dataset. VTAMLST also contains lists of start options and lists of major nodes to be activated at startup. The operator selects the desired options when VTAM is started.

Traditionally, VTAM tables had to be built manually before the network was started, and any change to the network required a change to the tables, which required VTAM to be stopped and re-started. This is now changing. The newer releases of VTAM that incorporate **APPN** capability also have the capability to change VTAMLST dynamically.

VTAM states

If you display a VTAM **node** it will be given a particular state. There are four types of VTAM state: inactive, **active**, going from inactive to active, and going from active to inactive. The last two types are the most interesting, and usually mean a **problem** of some description. The status usually starts with a P, meaning pending something. A lot of people refer to the state as 'pending'. Pending what? It is important to sort out whether the node is coming up or down to start with. You must then try to decipher exactly what the state means. You will require a VTAM messages and codes manual for this.

If a node is in a pending state of some description, something is waiting for something to happen. The problem diagnosis trick is to work out what the two somethings are. Unfortunately, that is your problem, although it does becomes easier with practice.

XIDs

XID is an **SDLC** command that is used to pass information between PUs. It is most commonly used at startup time when a PU does not know about the PU that is at the other end of a **link**. XIDs only carry information that relates to the PU.

X25

From an SNA point of view, X25 is simply a method of moving data between PUs. It performs exactly the same function as **SDLC**.

Most IBM communications hardware has the capability of supporting X25 if required. The considerations for choosing between SDLC and X25 are covered in the section on **SDLC or X25**.

See also the sections on **NPSI**, **QLLC** and **spoofing**.

3270 system

3270 refers to the terminal and **cluster controller** hardware system that is used for **mainframe** systems, and also for the commands and rules that are used to enable applications to work with terminals.

Thus we talk about 3270 terminals, 3270 applications, 3270 controllers and 3270 printers.

The 3174 is the current cluster controller. The 3274 is the older cluster controller. The only difference between the two boxes is features; they are both PU2s.

Note that there is no IBM piece of hardware with the number 3270.

5250 system

5250 refers to the terminal and **cluster controller** hardware system that is used for **S/3x** and **AS/400** systems, and also for the commands and rules that are used to enable applications to work with terminals.

Thus we talk about 5250 terminals, 5250 applications, 5250 controllers and 5250 printers.

Note that there is no IBM piece of hardware with the number 5250.

APPENDIX A
IBM MANUALS

IBM manuals are defined by their publication number. You will need to quote this to identify the manual. There is also an edition number that gives the latest edition. Ask for the most recent. This list is not exhaustive by any means, but gives some of the more useful manuals. All IBM manuals contain a list of related manuals, and this is often the best way to find additional useful material. This list is in no particular order.

GC30-3073 SNA Technical Overview
Definitions of most of the technical SNA terms. Contains a useful section on sequences.

GA27-3136 SNA Formats
Contains the format of the LH, TH, RH and RU for LU2 and LU6.2. This manual is extremely useful if you have to do debugging.

GA27-3093 Synchronous Data Link Control Concepts
Details of the SDLC protocol. The best place to start on SDLC.

GG24-3669 APPN Architecture and Implementations Tutorial
Quite a useful manual for those wanting to learn more about APPN.

SC30-3422 SNA Type 2.1 Node Reference
Technical detail on the T2.1 node architecture. Chapter 1 contains a good overview of the concepts.

GC30-3072 SNA Concepts and Products
Concentrates on the products.

SC30-3488 5394 Functions Reference
Contains details on the PU1, and also the 5250 commands. Useful for debugging in a 5250 environment.

GC31-6810 SAA Common Communications Support Summary
Easy to read and understand. Gives some interesting information on the communications bit of SAA.

Appendix A

SC21-9601 AS/400 Communications Users' Guide
A very useful manual for working in the AS/400 environment. It contains all the parameter settings for the communications part of the operating system.

GA23-0218 3174 Functional Description
A useful manual. Details of the 3174 functionality and the 3270 datastream. Some of this manual is also relevant to the 3274.

GC20-1868 SNA Format and Protocol Reference Manual
Detailed information on hierarchical SNA. Very technical and heavy.

SC30-3562 SNA Format and Protocol Architectural Logic for LU6.2
Technical detail for dependent LU6.2.

SC31-6808 SNA LU6.2 Reference: Peer Protocols
Technical detail for independent LU6.2.

GG24-3649 IBM Telecommunication Products Implementation Guide
Lots of examples of mainframe system generations for all types of communications product.

Appendix B

APPENDIX B
COMMON SEQUENCES

SDLC startup

This sequence illustrates the SDLC command flow when starting a link between a PU4 and a PU2.

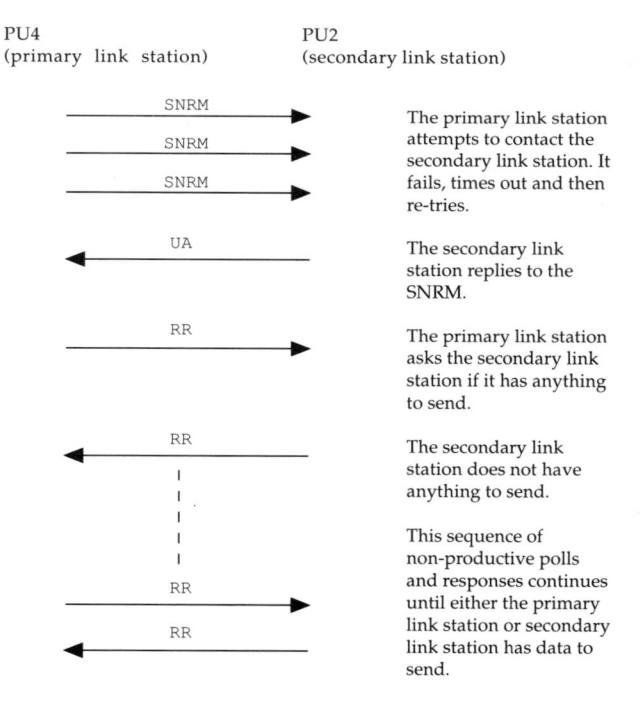

```
PU4                            PU2
(primary link station)         (secondary link station)

          SNRM
    ───────────────▶           The primary link station
          SNRM                 attempts to contact the
    ───────────────▶           secondary link station. It
          SNRM                 fails, times out and then
    ───────────────▶           re-tries.

          UA
    ◀───────────────           The secondary link
                               station replies to the
                               SNRM.

          RR
    ───────────────▶           The primary link station
                               asks the secondary link
                               station if it has anything
                               to send.

          RR
    ◀───────────────           The secondary link
         |                     station does not have
         |                     anything to send.
         |
         |                     This sequence of
         |                     non-productive polls
          RR                   and responses continues
    ───────────────▶           until either the primary
          RR                   link station or secondary
    ◀───────────────           link station has data to
                               send.
```

X25 QLLC

This sequence illustrates QLLC with incoming call and switched virtual circuit. It uses AS/400 and 5394 as an example.

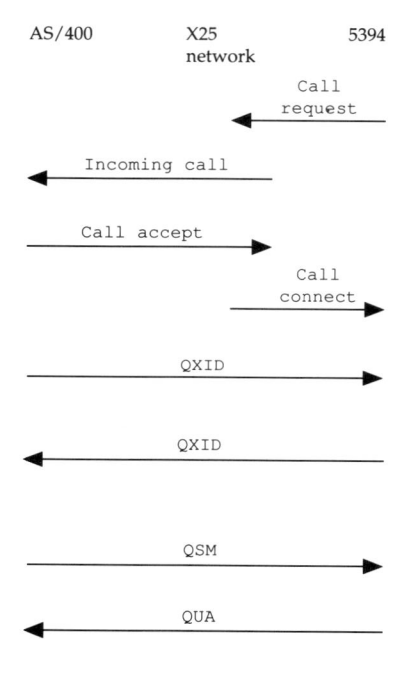

```
AS/400           X25              5394
                 network
                           Call
                        ◄──request──

          ◄──Incoming call──

          ──Call accept──►

                           Call
                         ──connect──►              The SVC between the AS/400 and
                                                   5394 is now established.

          ──────QXID──────►                        The AS/400 requests on XID from
                                                   the 5394. This is sent in a qualified
                                                   packet.

          ◄─────QXID──────                         The 5394 replies with its XID.
                                                   The AS/400 tries to match the
                                                   IDNUM and IDBLK numbers. If it
                                                   succeeds . . .

          ──────QSM───────►                        The AS/400 sends a SNRM in a
                                                   qualified packet.

          ◄─────QUA───────                         The 5394 replies with a UA in a
                                                   qualified packet.

                                                   The connection between AS/400
                                                   and 5394 is now operational.
```

Appendix B

Activation sequence 5250 systems

This sequence illustrates the SNA command flow when a 5250 cluster controller is brought up. It includes the SDLC startup sequence.

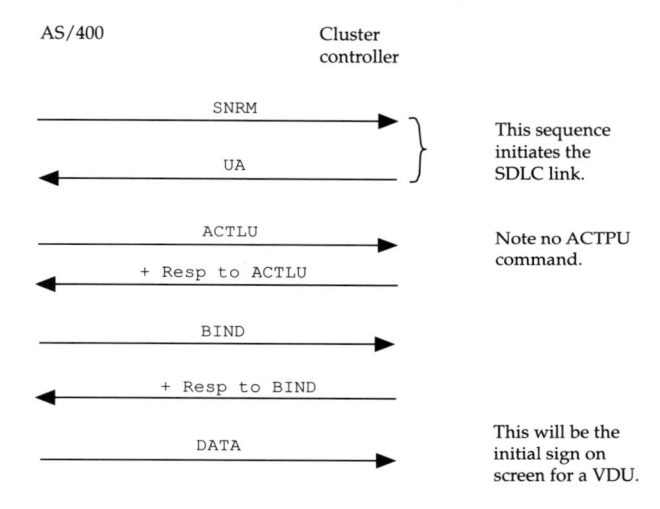

```
AS/400                      Cluster
                            controller

            SNRM
    ───────────────────▶  ⎫
                          ⎬   This sequence
            UA            ⎭   initiates the
    ◀───────────────────       SDLC link.

           ACTLU
    ───────────────────▶      Note no ACTPU
                              command.
        + Resp to ACTLU
    ◀───────────────────

            BIND
    ───────────────────▶

        + Resp to BIND
    ◀───────────────────

            DATA              This will be the
    ───────────────────▶      initial sign on
                              screen for a VDU.
```

Appendix B

Activation sequence 3270 system

This sequence illustrates the SNA command flow when a 3270 cluster controller is brought up. It assumes that the link has been successfully started.

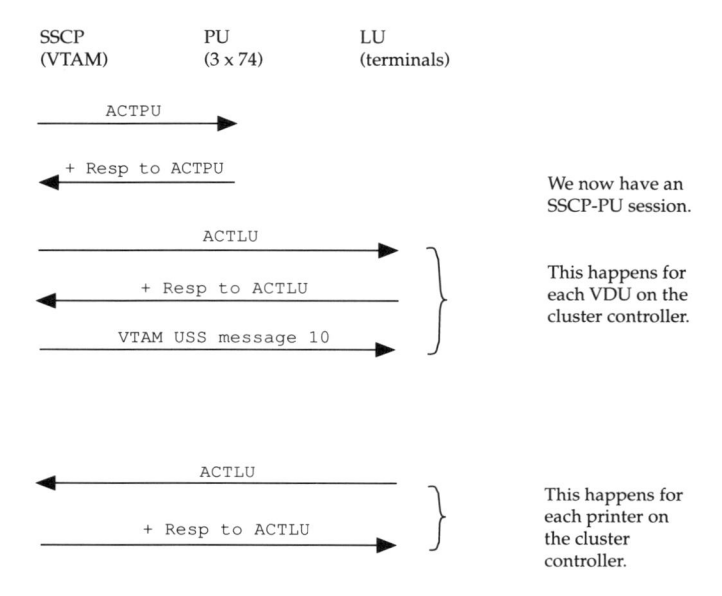

```
SSCP              PU              LU
(VTAM)          (3 x 74)       (terminals)

      ACTPU
   ─────────►

      + Resp to ACTPU
   ◄─────────────                      We now have an
                                       SSCP-PU session.

              ACTLU
           ─────────────►
                                    ⎫
              + Resp to ACTLU       ⎪  This happens for
           ◄─────────────           ⎬  each VDU on the
                                    ⎪  cluster controller.
              VTAM USS message 10   ⎪
           ─────────────►           ⎭


              ACTLU
           ◄─────────────
                                    ⎫  This happens for
              + Resp to ACTLU       ⎬  each printer on
           ─────────────►           ⎪  the cluster
                                    ⎭  controller.
```

Appendix B

Terminal user initiates the activation of an LU-LU session

This sequence illustrates the data flow when a 3270 terminal user logs on to an application.

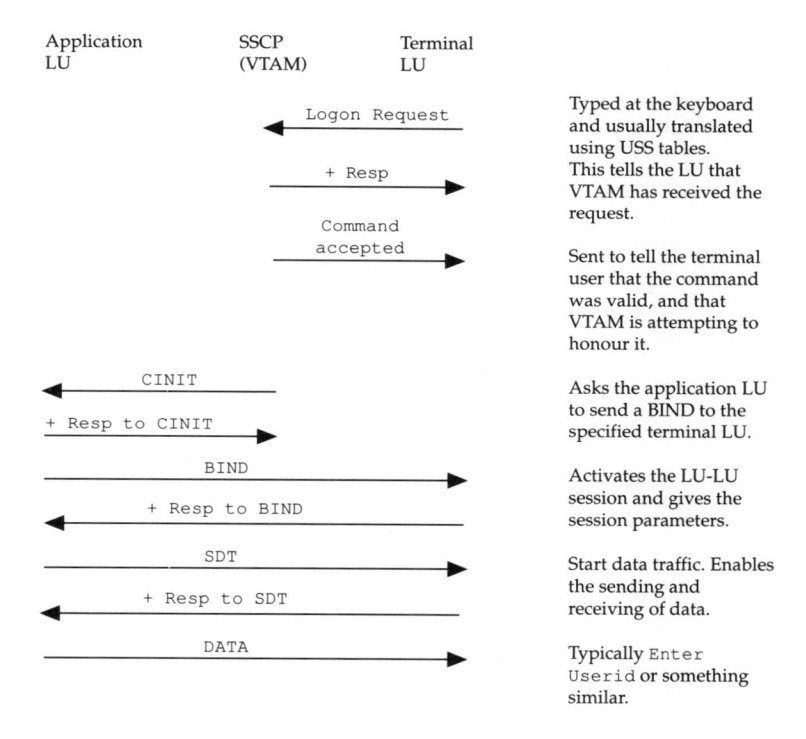

Application LU	SSCP (VTAM)	Terminal LU	
	← Logon Request		Typed at the keyboard and usually translated using USS tables. This tells the LU that VTAM has received the request.
	+ Resp →		
	Command accepted →		Sent to tell the terminal user that the command was valid, and that VTAM is attempting to honour it.
← CINIT			Asks the application LU to send a BIND to the specified terminal LU.
+ Resp to CINIT →			
BIND →			Activates the LU-LU session and gives the session parameters.
← + Resp to BIND			
SDT →			Start data traffic. Enables the sending and receiving of data.
← + Resp to SDT			
DATA →			Typically Enter Userid or something similar.

Application program initiates the activation of an LU-LU session

This sequence illustrates the data flow when an application program initiates the activation of an LU-LU session. The application could be printing or a network solicitor, the sequence will be identical in either case. Note that from the CINIT on, the sequence is the same as the previous example.

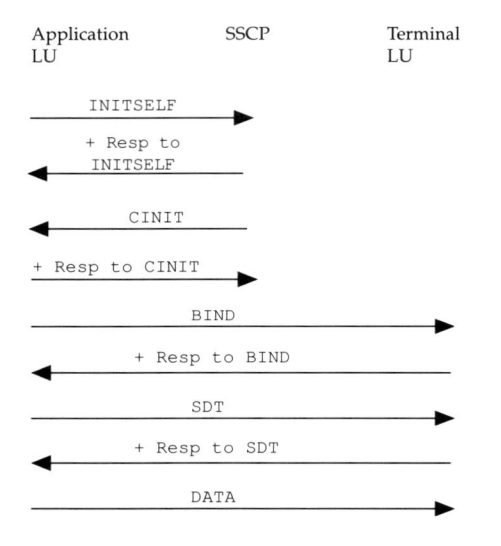

```
Application            SSCP             Terminal
LU                                      LU

      INITSELF
    ─────────────►
     + Resp to
    ◄─── INITSELF

             CINIT
    ◄─────────────
    + Resp to CINIT
    ─────────────►

              BIND
    ─────────────────────────────────►
             + Resp to BIND
    ◄─────────────────────────────────

              SDT
    ─────────────────────────────────►
             + Resp to SDT
    ◄─────────────────────────────────

              DATA
    ─────────────────────────────────►
```

Sent to ask the SSCP to assist in activating the session.

Asks the application LU to send a BIND to the specified terminal LU.

Activates the LU-LU session and gives the session parameters.

Start data traffic. Enables the sending and receiving of data.

Appendix B

Terminal user initiates the activation of a cross-domain LU-LU session

This sequence illustrates the data flow when a 3270 terminal user logs on to an application in another domain. SSCP(A) indicates the application's SSCP, and SSCP(T) indicates the terminal's SSCP. The positive responses are not included for clarity.

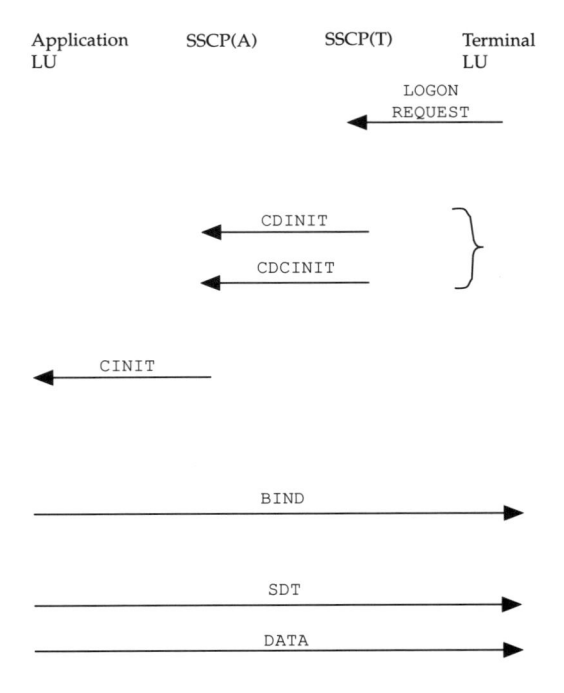

```
Application      SSCP(A)        SSCP(T)        Terminal
LU                                              LU
                                 LOGON
                             ◄── REQUEST ───
```
SSCP(T) realizes that the requested LU is not in its domain.

```
                ◄── CDINIT ───
                ◄── CDCINIT ──
```
These commands say 'I have this LU in my domain which wants an LU-LU session with this LU in your domain'.

```
  ◄── CINIT ───
```
Exactly the same CINIT as the single domain example. The application knows nothing of where the other LU is.

```
  ─────────── BIND ──────────────►
```
The BIND command will not flow through SSCP(T) if the terminal is connected as in Fig. 10.

```
  ─────────── SDT ───────────────►
  ─────────── DATA ──────────────►
```

APPENDIX C
COMMON IBM
COMMUNICATIONS HARDWARE

This appendix lists some of the IBM communications hardware with a brief description. The list is not exhaustive and does not include terminals.

3044 fibreoptic channel extender
3174 newer 3270 cluster controller
3274 older 3270 cluster controller
3705 older communication controller
3708 protocol converter
3720 newer smaller communication controller
3721 expansion unit for 3720
3725 older communication controller
3737 channel-to-channel unit
3745 newer larger communication controller
3746 expansion unit for 3745
3767 SDLC device with keyboard and printer
5294 older 5250 cluster controller
5395 newer 5250 cluster controller
5494 cluster controller for AS/400
5853 modem
6611 multiprotocol router
7861 modem
7868 modem
8230 token ring wiring concentrator
9715 integrated access multiplexer
9736 bandwidth manager
9738 bandwidth manager

APPENDIX D
COMMON SNA COMMANDS

This appendix lists the more common SNA commands and their purpose.

LUSTAT
Sent from LU to LU or SSCP, it is used to send 4 bytes of status information.

ACTLU
Sent from the SSCP to LU, it activates an SSCP-LU session and establishes session parameters.

DACTLU
Sent from the SSCP to LU, it de-activates an SSCP-LU session. The command is either 1 or 3 bytes long.

ACTPU
Sent from the SSCP to the PU, it activates the SSCP-PU session.

DACTPU
Sent from the SSCP to the PU, it de-activates an SSCP-PU session.

ACTCDRM
Sent from one SSCP to another, it activates an SSCP-SSCP session, and exchanges information.

DACTCDRM
Sent from SSCP to SSCP, it de-activates the SSCP-SSCP session.

BIND
Sent from PLU to SLU or CP to CP, it contains the session parameters. It activates the LU-LU or CP-CP session.

UNBIND
Sent from LU to LU, it de-activates the session between the two LUs.

SDT
Start data traffic is sent from the PLU to the SLU. It initiates the sending of data requests and responses.

RSHUTD
Request shutdown is sent from the SLU to the PLU. It indicates that the SLU is ready to have the LU-LU session de-activated. The expected response from the PLU is UNBIND.

ACTLINK
Sent from SSCP to PU type 4. It initiates the link contact procedures.

DACTLINK
Sent from SSCP to PU type 4. It initiates the procedure to disconnect the link.

REQDISCONT
Sent from PU to SSCP. It requests that the SSCP starts the procedure which ultimately results in the discontact of the PU.

CONTACTED
Sent from PU type 4 to the SSCP. It indicates the completion of the data link layer contact procedure, i.e. for SDLC links, an SNRM has been sent and a UA received.

TERMSELF
Sent from the LU to the SSCP, it requests that the SSCP assists in the termination of LU-LU sessions between the OLU and the specified DLU.

NMVT
Sent between SSCP and PU, it carries management services data in the form of MS vectors.

CINIT
Sent from SSCP to PLU, it requests that the PLU activates a session using a BIND request.

NOTIFY
Sent between the SSCP and LU, or between two SSCPs, it carries status information.

Appendix D

CDINIT
Sent from SSCP to SSCP, it requests that the SSCP(DLU) assists in starting a session between the specified LUs.

CDCINIT
Sent from SSCP to SSCP, it passes information about the SLU to the SSCP(PLU) and requests that the SSCP(PLU) sends a CINIT to the PLU.